Officers

at

Arnhem

An Examination of the Command Structure of the British 1st Airborne Division Which Fought at Arnhem in September 1944

TRAVELOGUE 219

Trevor Laing

TL219-309 Officers at Arnhem, July 2015 compiled by Trevor Laing
Published by: Travelogue 219
           Toronto, Canada
           www.tl219.com

ISBN 978-1-927679-30-2

Second Edition

Front cover photo:

top: Divisional Headquarters taken in the summer of 1944

middle: a glider comes into land during training.

bottom left: Lt. Comper listens to General Weeks at a reunion of Canloan officers after the war.

Bottom right: Canloan officers Lieutenants Harvie and Turner

Contents

Introduction

The following is a list of officers in the British 1st Airborne Division who fought at Arnhem during Operation Market Garden and this book is designed not only as a quick reference, but also to give an idea of the command structure, history and function of every unit in the division.

The war establishment for an Airborne Division in 1944 lists the strength of the division at 11,770 total ranks, which included 668 officers, 129 Warrant Officers, 831 Sergeants, 1,161 Corporals and 8,981 Privates. We know that they weren't at full strength and that the division didn't always keep to the war establishment tables, so the figure is much lower. Also, the entire division didn't participate in Operation Market Garden so the number of officers who flew to Arnhem is much lower than 668.

I've included warrant officers in the list of officers of the British 1st Airborne Division who landed in The Netherlands during Operation Market Garden and even the occasional Sergeant who held an officer's posting. Where possible I have included the man's year of birth and, if they have passed away, the year of his death and any awards that he received during the war. When not specified all dates are assumed to be September 1944.

Please realize that the notes on who returned from Arnhem are for those who were evacuated during Operation Berlin and not for those who were evaders or escaped as prisoners of war.

I would like to believe that the list is 100% complete and accurate, but if you have more information and/or corrections please contact me via the publisher.

Divisional Command Post

Divisional Headquarters

Led by a Major-General, the divisional headquarters' Operation Branch was able to control the fighting element of the division while the Adjutant General Staff controlled the division's logistics. The Air Branch coordinated with the air force for transport and re-supply. The war establishment for 17 September 1944 listed 35 officers and 157 other ranks with 34 motorcycles, 34 vehicles and 27 trailers. Only 20 Officers and 142 other ranks went to Arnhem and only 13 Officers — including the General and his aide — and 28 other ranks returned.

Major General Robert Elliot `Roy' Urquhart,
General Officer Commanding
1901-1988

Captain Graham Chatfield **Roberts**, Aide-de-Camp
1914-1985

General Staff Branch:

Operations Branch:

General Staff Officer 1:	Lieutenant-Colonel Charles Baillie **Mackenzie** DSO 1909-1991
General Staff Officer 2:	Major Owen Frank **Newton-Dunn** 1911—1995
General Staff Officer 3:	Captain Charles Gordon **Grieve**

Air Branch:

General Staff Officer 2:	Major David John **Madden**. He was killed in action on September 21st, 1944 at the age of 25.
General Staff Officer 3:	Captain D.W. **McCombe**

Intelligence Branch:

General Staff Officer 2:	Major Hugh Pownall **Maguire** 1912-1997
General Staff Officer 3:	Captain Charles Peter **Scott-Malden** 1914-1972
General Staff Officer:	Captain P.A.H. **Hodgson** 1921-2002

Adjutant & Quartermaster (A&Q) Branch:
Assistant A&Q General: Lieutenant-Colonel Philip Henry
Herbert **Preston**, OBE
Deputy Assistant Quartermaster General: Major Ernest Rupert
Hodges 1920 -
Deputy Assistant Adjutant General: Major Lawrence Kent
Hardman MiD 1913-1988
Services:
Ass.Dir. of Medical Services:Colonel Graeme Mathhaw **Warrack**
OBE, DSO 1913-1985
Dep. Ass. Dir. of Medical Services: Major Joseph Esmond **Miller**
MC 1914-1990
Ass. Dir. of Ordnance Services: Lt-Col. Gerald Hubrey **Mobbs**
1911-1976
Assistant Provost Marshal: Major Oliver Peter **Haig** 1908-1987
Deputy Assistant Provost Marshal: Captain Ernest **Deuchar**
MC, MiD 1911-1995
Senior Chaplin: Major A.H.W. **Harlow**

1st Airborne Division Headquarters Defense and Employment Platoon:

Formed from the Oxford and Bucks Light Infantry and consisted of an anti aircraft Section*, two ground defense section and 2 employment sections, this platoon was responsible for the defense and administration of the Divisional Headquarters.

Commanding Officer: Lieutenant Alfred David **Butterworth**
1921-1994

* AA section did not go to Arnhem

89th Parachute Field Security Section

This unit's duties include interpretation, interrogation of prisoners, maintaining security measures and the dissemination of intelligence. One officer and 18 other ranks landed at Arnhem and only five men returned.

Commanding Officer: Captain Sir John Edward **Killick**
1919-2004

Sergeant Major: W.O.II T.E. **Armstrong**

Provost Marshal's 1st Airborne Div.

This small group of men was responsible for traffic control, directing lost personnel back to their units, collecting prisoners from forward units to the rear and maintaining discipline in the division area. Of the 5 officers and 76 other ranks who landed at Arnhem only 1 officer (Major Haig) and 11 men returned.

Assistant Provost Marshal: Major Oliver Peter **Haig**
1908-1987

Deputy Ass. Provost Marshal: Captain Ernest **Deuchar**
MC, MiD 1911-1995

1st Airborne Provost Company

Commanding Officer: Captain William Buchanan **Gray**
He died of wounds on September 29th at the age of 31.

Regimental Sergeant Major: W.O.I W. **Kibble**

Commander No. 1 Provost
Section (1 Para Bde): Captain Wilfred David `Wilf'
Clarence **Morley** 1920-1995

Commander No 2 Provost
Section (4 Para. Bde.): Lt. Thomas Joseph Arthur **Smith**

Commander No. 3 Provost
Section (1 A/L Bde): Lt. Frank Lewis **Horton**
1924-

Commander No. 4 Provost
Section (Div. HQ): Lt. Rudolph J. **Falck**. He went missing on September 25th and has no known grave.

The Brigades

The brigades were the main fighting component of the division. Two brigades were delivered to the battlefield by parachute while the third landed in gliders.

Typical Parachute Brigade:

- Headquarters

- 3 x Parachute Battalions

    - Headquarters

    - Headquarters Company

    - Support Company

    - 3 x Parachute Companies

Typical Airlanding Brigade:

- Headquarters

- 3 x Airlanding Battalions

    - Headquarters

    - Headquarters Company

    - Support Company

    - 4 x Infantry Companies

1 Parachute Brigade

This unit was the original parachute brigade of all of Britain's airborne forces and was the most experienced in the division. The war establishment for a Parachute Headquarters, effective March 1943, lists 11 Officers and 44 Other Ranks with 20 motor-cycles and 7 vehicles and doesn't include the Defence Platoon and the attached officers listed below. Three Chaplains are part of its war establishment, but are listed with the battalion to which they were attached. Of the 13 officers and 69 other ranks that made up the brigade headquarters only 1 officer (Captain Taylor) and 2 men returned.

Headquarters

Commanding Officer: Brigadier Sir Gerald William `Legs' **Lathbury**,DSO,MBE,DSC 1906-1978

Staff:

Brigade Major: Major James Anthony **Hibbert** MC 1917-

Intelligence and Gas Duties: Captain Willie Andrew **Taylor** 1921-2000

General Staff Officer 3 (Air): Captain Cecil Ralph **Miller**

Deputy Assistant Adjutant Major Cecil Distin **Byng-Maddick**
Quartermaster General: MBE 1919-2006

Services:

Captain (parachute duties): Captain Bernard Walter **Briggs** MC 1919-1985

Brigade RASC Officer: Captain Douglas Gerald **Mortlock** 1920-

Brigade Signals Officer: Captain Wilfred James **Marquand**

Second in Command (HQ): Lieutenant John Brown **Cairns** 1923-

Medical Officer: Captain David **Wright**, MC BK

Commander Defence Pl: Lieutenant John Partrick **Barnett** BL 1908-1992

Liaison Officer 2 Para Bn.: Lieutenant Andrew **Roberts**

Liaison Officer 3 Para Bn.: Lieutenant Henry Stanley **Dean** DCM 1918-2011

1st Battalion, The Parachute Regiment

Formed from volunteers after Dunkirk, the original members of the battalion were Britain's very first parachute troops. After being No. 2 Commando with a Guards' troop and then the 11th SAS, it became the 1st Battalion, The Parachute Regiment, in September 1941. After heavy losses in Tunisia replacements came from the 10th Royal Welsh Fusiliers after it had formed the 6th Battalion, The Parachute Regiment. This gave the battalion a Guards and Welsh character. Thirty-four officers and 548 other ranks landed at Arnhem and only 3 officers and 101 men returned.

Headquarters

Commanding Officer:	Lt-Col. David Theodor **Dobie** DSO, RMWO 1912-1971
Second in Command:	Major John Cuthbert **Bune** 1914-17.09.44
Adjutant:	Captain Philip Nigel **Groves** 1918-2010
Assistant Adjutant:	Lt. Alastair Duncan **Clarkson** 1922– 22.09.44
Transport Officer:	Lt. John Liewellyn **Williams** DSO
Intelligence Officer:	Lt. Vladmir Alexandrovitch **Britneff** 1919-1994
Commander 1st Glider Party:	Lt. Leslie Arthur **Curtiss** MM 1919-20.09.44 NKG
Commander 2nd Glider Party:	Lt. Albert Thomas **Turrell** BC 1919 -
Medical Officer:	Captain Arthur **Percival** MiD 1916-2000
Regimental Sergeant Major:	W.O.I H.A. **Eatwell**
Attached:	Lt. Leo Jack **Heaps** MC 1922-1996

Headquarters / Support Company

Officer Commanding: Captain John Alan Emlyn **Davies** 1909-1997

Company Sergeant Major: W.O.II E.G.B. **Martin**

Commander Assault Platoon: Lietenant William John Fisher **Sutton** 1920-1998

Commander Signals Platoon: Lieutenant James Joseph-**Lasenby** 1916-1999

Commander Mortar Platoon: Lieutenant George Edmund **Guyon** 1916-2000

Commander Medium Machine Gun Platoon: Lieutenant Joseph **Gardiner**, MiD

Quartermaster: Lieutenant Thomas **Brown**

RQMS: W.O.II J.R. **Nicholson**

R Company

Officer Commanding: Major John **Timothy**, MC 1914-2011

Second in Command: Capt. Peter Geoffrey Alan **Mansfield** 1919-1990

Company Sergeant Major: W.O.II J. **Whitley**

Commander No. 1 Platoon: Lt. Frederick Henry **Greenhalgh**

Commander No. 2 Platoon: Lieutenant Michael G. **Kilmartin** He was killed on the 19th and has no known grave.

Commander No. 3 Platoon: Lt. Richard Angus **Halstead** MC 1917-1977

S Company

Officer Commanding: Major Ronald Leslie **Stark**
MC, MiD, BL 1913-1990

Second in Command: Captain John Charles **O'Sullivan**
1914-1988

Company Sergeant Major: W.O. II L.E. **Oxley**, DCM

Commander No. 5 Platoon: Lieutenant B.J. **Glick**

Commander No. 6 Platoon: Lieutenant Richard Arthur James
Bingley 1920-2002

Commander No. 7 Platoon: Lieutenant Robert Harold Bruce
Feltham 1923-2001

T Company

Officer Commanding: Major Christopher **Perrin-Brown**
MC DSO 1917-1995

Second in Command: Captain James Alexander Dodwell
Richey 1910-1997

Company Sergeant Major: W.O.II A.J. **King**, MiD

Commander No. 9 Platoon: Lieutenant John T. **McFadden**. He
died as a prisoner of war from Polio
on Oct. 4th 1944 at the age of 28.

Commander No.10 Pl.: Lieutenant Eric J. **Davies**
MC MiD 1918-2005

Commander No.11 Pl.: Lieutenant John Edward **Helingoe**
BL 1923-1996

2nd Battalion, The Parachute Regiment

Formed on October 1st, 1941, the battalion had a strong Scottish and Irish presence. One of its companies successfully carried out the famous Bruneval Raid. At Arnhem there were 31 officers and 495 other ranks, of which only 17 other ranks returned.

Headquarters

Commanding Officer: Lt-Col. John Dulton **Frost** DSO, MC 1912-1993

Second in Command: Major David W. **Wallis** MiD. He was killed on the 18th at the age of 29.

Adjutant: Captain Donald W. **McLean** 1925-2001

Intelligence Officer: Lt. Clifford D. **Boiteaux-Buchanan** He was killed on the 20th.

Liaison Officer: 2Lt. James Sydney Channel **Flavell** 1924-2008

Medical Officer: Captain James Watt **Logan** DSO BL

Chaplain: Captain Bernard Mary **Egan** MC 1905-1988

Regimental Sergeant Major: W.O.I G.A. **Strachan**

Headquarters Company

Officer Commanding: Major Francis R. **Tate.** He was killed on 21st at the age of 39.

Commander Signals Platoon: Lt. John Graham **Blunt** 1916-1997

Administration Officers: Lt. John Thomspon **Ainsite** 1918-1998

Lt. A.L. **Tannenbaum**

Company Sergeant Major: W.O.II J.E. **Bishop**

Commander Assault Platoon: Lt. Donald Marsh **Douglas** 1919-2003

Support Company

Officer Commanding: Captain Stanley Charles **Panter** MC 1909-1968

Commander Mortar Platoon: Lt. R.B. **Woods** He died of wounds on October 14th, 1944 at the age of 25.

Commander Medium Machine Gun Platoon: Lt. John Humphrey Arnold **Monsell** 1916-1989

A Company

Officer Commanding: Major Allison Digby **Tatham-Warter** DSO 1917-1993

Second in Command: Captain Anthony Mutrie **Frank** MC MiD SS 1917-2008

Company Sergeant Major: W.O.II Dennis **Meads** He was killed on the 18th at the age of 25.

Commander No. 1 Platoon: Lt. Robert Alexander **Viasto** 1924-2003

Commander No. 2 Platoon: Lt. John H. **Grayburn** VC. He was killed on the 20th at the age of 26.

Commander No. 3 Platoon: Lt. A.J. **McDermont** He was killed on the 22nd at the age of 25.

B Company

Officer Commanding: Major Douglas Edward **Crawley** MC 1920-1986

Second in Command: Captain Francis Kinglake **Hoyer-Millar**, MC 1919-1993

Company Sergeant Major: W.O.II William W. **Scott**. He was killed on either the 20th or the 25th.

Commander No. 4 Platoon: Lt. Robert Hugh **Levien** 1919-2004

Commander No. 5 Platoon: Lt. Colin Macdonald **Stanford** 1923-

Commander No. 6 Platoon: Lt. Peter H. **Cane.** He was killed on the 17th at the age 25.

C Company

Officer Commanding: Major Victor **Dover**, MC 1919-1982

Second in Command: Captain Richard Elwin **Morton** 1917-1997

Company Sergeant Major: W.O.II D.R. **Tasker**

Commander No. 7 Platoon: Lt. David Edward Charles **Russell** 1923-2013

Commander No. 8 Platoon: Lt. John Alexander **Russell** MiD 1922-98

Commander No. 9 Platoon: Lt. Philip Hambury **Barry** 1923-2011

3rd Battalion, The Parachute Regiment

Formed in October 1941 and unlike the other two battalions in the brigade, it never had any regional characteristics. It was the first British parachute battalion to land as a complete unit when it dropped onto Bone airfield in North Africa. Twenty-seven officers and 567 other ranks landed at Arnhem. Only 1 officer and 34 other ranks returned.

Headquarters

Commanding Officer: Lt.-Col. John A.C. **Fitch**. He was killed on the 19th at the age of 32.

Second in Command: Major Alan **Bush**, MC 1918-1998

Adjutant: Captain Ernest Walter **Seccombe** 1913-1974

Intelligence Officer: Lt. Alexis Peter **Vedeniapine** MM, BL 1916-1991

Liaison Officer: Lt. William A. **Fraser** He was killed on the 20th.

Medical Officer: Captain John **Rutherford** MC SS 1915-1988

Chaplain: Capt. Edward Leigh **Philips** 1912-

Regimental Sergeant Major: W.O.I J.C. **Lord**, MBE

Headquarters / Support Company

Officer Commanding: Major James I. **Houston**. He was killed on the 20th at the age of 32 and has no known grave.

Company Sergeant Major: W.O.II J. **Seeckts**

Commander Assault Platoon: Lt. B.H.D. **Burwash** MC 1916-1979

Commander Signals Platoon: Lt. John Pryce 1915-1987

Commander Mortar Platoon: Lt. S. **Gillespie**

Commander Medium Machine Gun Platoon: Lt. Milton Jon Patrick Stanley **Dickson** 1921-1996

A.P.T.C. Instructor: W.O.II E. **Innes**

A Company

Officer Commanding: Major Mervyn William **Dennison** MC 1914-1993

Second in Command: Captain Roderic Miles Doughty **Thessiger** 1915-2005

Company Sergeant Major: W.O.II A. **Watson**

Commander No. 1 Platoon: Lt. Raymond M. **Bussell**. He was murdered on October 10th, 1944 by the SS for wearing civilian clothes.

Commander No. 2 Platoon: Lt. Anthony Rysing **Baxter** 1921-2005

Commander No. 3 Platoon: Lt. Bertram Percival **Ash** 1912-1989

B Company

Officer Commanding: Major Alexander Peter H. **Waddy**. He was killed on the 18th at the age of 25.

Second in Command: Captain Geoffrey R. **Dorrien-Smith**. He was killed on the 21st.

Company Sergeant Major: W.O.II R. **Allen**, DSC. He was killed on the 19th.

Commander No. 4 Platoon: Lt. Ernest Albert **James** MC MiD 1913-2011

Commander No. 5 Platoon: Lt. Sir James Arnold Stacey **Cleminson**, MC MiD 1921-2010

Commander No. 6 Platoon: Lt. Gordon Trevor **Hill**. He was killed on the 18th at the age of 26.

C Company

Officer Commanding: Major Richard Peter Cecil **Lewis** MiD 1915-1985

Second in Command: Captain Sir Wilfred Henry Frederick **Robinson** 1917-2012

Company Sergeant Major: W.O.II A. **Day**

Commander No. 7 Platoon: Lt. Peter **Hibburt**. He was killed on the 18th at the age of 21.

Commander No. 8 Platoon: Lt. Gerald Maurice **Infield** 1921-

Commander No. 9 Platoon: Lt. Leonard William **Wright**

4th Parachute Brigade

It formed as an independent brigade in the Middle East in 1942 and transferred to the division in 1943. Arnhem was its first action as a brigade. Of the headquarters' 16 officers and 68 men, only 2 officers and 15 other ranks returned.

Headquarters

Commanding Officer:	Brigadier John W. `Shan' **Hackett** DSO MBE, MC MiD
Brigade Major:	Major Charles N.B. **Dawson** MC, MiD. He was killed on the 20th at the age of 27.
Intelligence and Gas Duties Officer:	Captain George M. **Blundell.** He was killed on the 20th at the age of 27.
General Staff Officer 3:	Captain Reginald Robert **Temple** SS 1922-2009
Deputy Ass. Adjutant QM:	Captain **Barrow** (not at Arnhem)
Staff Captain:	Captain Herbert Brian **Booty** 1919-2005
Brigade RASC Officer:	Captain Colin Reid **Harkess** MiD 1912-2008
Brigade Signals Officer:	Captain Alan Bishop **Kennet** 1920-
Medical Officer:	Captain Richard Erskine **Bonham-Carter** 1910-1994
Commander Defence Platoon:	Lt. H. G. **Taylor** (not at Arnhem)
Liaison Officer 156 Para.Bn.:	Lt. Frederick John de Riveille **Locke**
Liaison Officer 10 Para Bn.:	Lt. Harold Theodore Bernhardt **Matthews** 1918-
Liaison Officer 11 Para Bn.:	Lt. W.H. **Sackville**, Lord Buckhurst
Cdr. 6th LAD R.E.M.E	Lt. Archibald May **Brodie** 1919-
Bde. Transportation Officer:	Captain Derek John **Taylor** 1920-
Sergeant Major:	W.O. II W. **Hennon**
Attached:	Captain E.D. **James.** He was killed on the 20th at the age of 26.

156th Battalion, the Parachute Regiment

It was originally the 151 Battalion, which was raised in India in October 1941, and was renumbered to fool the enemy intelligence to believe that it was a new unit. Of its 31 officer and 513 other ranks, only 3 officers and 56 men returned.

Headquarters

Commanding Officer: Lt.-Col.– Sir William Richard de Bacquencourt **des Voeux**, Bt, MiD. He was killed on the 20th at the age of 32.

Second in Command: Major Ernest V. **Ritson**, MiD. He was killed on the 20th at the age of 35.

Adjutant: Captain Frederick Michael **Gibbs** 1920-1999

Intelligence Officer: Lt. Hon. O.P. St. **Aubyn** MiD MC

Medical Officer: Captain John Edward **Buck** 1915-2006

Chaplain: Captain Alistair Charles Vass **Menzies** 1916-2005

Liaison Officer French Army: Lt. Yves **Hacart.** He was killed on the 18th at the age of 33.

Regimental Sergeant Major: W.O.I R.D. **Gay** DCM

Headquarters Company

Officer Commanding: Major Michael **Page**, MiD. He was killed on the 20th at the age of 33.

Second in Command: Captain Vernon John Ballis **Silverster** 1915-1985

Commander Signals Platoon: Lt. Douglas John **Suter** 1921-

Liaison Officer: Lt. Victor Ray **Twidle** 1915-2010

Quartermaster: Lt. Thomas Graham **Bush,** MBE 1919-1983

Regt. Quartermaster Sgt.: W.O.II Reginald G. **Badger.** He was killed on the 18th at age 26.

Instructor A.P.T.C.: W.O.II N. **McKinnon**

Company Sergeant Major: Sergeant E. **Read**

Support Company

Officer Commanding: Captain Thomas James **Wainwright** BC MiD

Second in Command: Captain James Bianco **Clegg** MC 1917-08

Company Sergeant Major: W.O.II Ronald McCardie Martin **Chenery**, BC 1922-2011

Commander Mortar Platoon Lt. R.M.M. **Adams**

Commander Medium MG Pl.: Lt. Jeffrey Fraser **Noble** 1923-

Command Anti Tank Platoon: Lt. Harry M.A. **Cambier**, MiD. He was murdered 10-10-1944 at the age of 23 while wearing civilian clothes.

A Company

Officer Commanding: Major Robert Laslett John **Pott** MC 1919-2005

Second in Command: Captain Terence P.W. **Rogers**. He was killed on the 19th. He was 30.

Company Sergeant Major: W.O.II E.D. **Stroud**

Commander No. 1 Platoon: Sergeant W. **Griffiths**

Commander No. 2 Platoon: Lt. Stanley E. **Watling**, BEM. He was killed on the 19th. He was 28.

Commander No. 3 Platoon: Lt. Lindsay D. **Delacour**, MiD. He was killed on the 19th. He was 24.

B Company

Officer Commanding: Major John Liewellyn **Waddy** 1920

Second in Command: Captain H. **Montgomery**

Company Sergeant Major: W.O.II V.J. **Twist**

Commander No. 6 Platoon: Lt. Ronald W. **Wood**. He died of his wounds as a POW at the age of 28.

Commander No. 7 Platoon: Lt. John **Davison**. He was killed on the 18th at the age of 23.

Commander No. 8 Platoon: Lt. Dennis Benjamin **Kayne** 1921-1996

C Company

Officer Commanding: Major Geoffrey Stewart **Powell** MC 1919-2005

Second in Command: Captain J.J.M. **Kenyon-Bell**

Company Sergeant Major: W.O.II W.S. **Sykes**, BEM

Commander No. 9 Platoon: Lt. N.R. **Willock**

Commander No. 10 Platoon: (acting Lt.) Sgt. J.A. **Black**

Commander No. 11 Platoon: Lt. William S. **Donaldson**. He was killed on the 20th at the age of 25.

10th Battalion, The Parachute Regiment

It was raised in December 1942 at Kabrit from recruits mostly from the British 8th Army. A third of them came from the Royal Sussex and an effort was made to attract officers from the regiment. The Commanding Officer was from South Wales Borderers, but his RSM was Royal Sussex. None of the officers and only 92 other ranks of the 31 officers and 571 other ranks that landed at Arnhem returned to the UK in 1944.

Headquarters

Commanding Officer: Lt-Col. Kennth B.I. **Smyth** OBE, MiD. He died of wounds on the 30th at the age of 38.

Second in Command: Major George G. **Widdowson** 1911-2002

Adjutant: Captain Nickolas Brian **Hanmer** 1921-2003

Intelligence Officer: Lt. John M. **Henry**. He was killed on the 19th at the age of 23.

Brigade Liaison Officer: Lt. H.C.J. **Roderick**. He was killed on the 18th at the age of 24.

Medical Officer: Captain Gareth F.H. **Drayson**. He was killed on the 19th. He was 27.

Chaplain: Captain Raymond Franklin **Bowers** 1916-2001

Regimental Sergeant Major: W.O.I G. **White**

Headquarters Company

Officer Commanding: Major Charles F. **Ashoworth**. He was killed on either the 21st or 22nd at the age of 35.

Company Sergeant Major: W.O.II R. **Squire**

Instructor A.P.T.C.: W.O.II N. **Jones**

Commander Signals Pl.: Lt. John **Clarke**, MiD 1912-1991

Motor Transport Officer: Lt. Brian Dean **Carr** BL 1918-2004

Quartermaster: Lt. Joseph Winston **Glover** BS 1908-1996

Support Company

Officer Commanding: Major Francis William **Lindley** unknown-1982

Second in Command: Captain Dennis Dale **Smith**

Company Sergeant Major: W.O. II A.B. **Lashmore**

Commander Mortar Platoon: Lt. Roy G. W. **Dodd**. He was killed on the 20th. He was 30.

Commander Medium MG Pl.: Lt. Herbert C.N. **Radcliff**. He was killed on the 19th. He was 21.

Commander Anti Tank Pl.: Lt. Leslie Edward Sidney **Trehearn** 1913-1993

A Company

Officer Commanding: Major Patrick A.R. **Anson**. He died of wounds on the 29th as a POW.

Second in Command: Captain Lionel E. **Queripel**, VC. He was killed on the 19th. He was 24.

Company Sergeant Major: W.O.II G.H. **Lott**

Commander No. 3 Platoon: Lt. L.H.S. **Kiaer**. He was killed on the 20th at the age of 25.

Commander No. 4 Platoon: Lt. P.W.A. **Mackey**. He was killed on the 18th at the age of 24.

Commander No. 5 Platoon: Lt. John **Howard**. He drowned on October 20th, 1944.

B Company

Officer Commanding: Major Peter Esmond **Warr** MBE, DSO 1919-1982

Second in Command: Captain Benjamin Beattie **Clegg** MC 1918-1993

Company Sergeant Major: W.O.II T.J.E. **Courtie**

Commander No. 10 Platoon: LT. Albert Edwin **Baker** 1914-1975

Commander No. 11 Platoon: Lt. Michael Hugh **Broadway** 1920-2009

Commander No. 12 Platoon: Lt. William D.A. **Burgess**. He was killed on the 21st. He was 24.

C Company

Officer Commanding: Captain Cedric M. **Horsfall**. He has been missing since Sept. 20th 1944.

Second in Command: unknown

Company Sergeant Major: W.O.II R.E. **Grainger**, Mi, BS

Commander No.16 Platoon: Lt. John Richard **Proctor**

Commander No. 17 Platoon: Lt. P.B. **MacKenzie**, DCM

Commander No. 18 Platoon: Lt. Peter **Saunders**, MiD KIA 22nd.

11th Battalion, The Parachute Regiment

Formed at Kabrit in March 1943 from a dwindling pool of volunteers and, unlike the other battalions, didn't fight in Italy. Its second Commanding Officer was formerly of the Lancashire Fusiliers. At Arnhem 31 officers and 556 other ranks landed and only 3 officers and 115 other ranks returned.

Headquarters

Commanding Officer: Lt-Col. Sir George Harris **Lea** 1912-1990

Second in Command: Major Richard Thomas Henry **Lonsdale**, DSO, MC 1913-1988

Adjutant: Captain Richard Alfred Godsal **Birchenough** 1921-1984

Intelligence Officer: Lt. William Patrick Cullen **Crawford**

Brigade Liaison Officer: Lt. Harry Ian **Bishop**

Medical Officer: Captain Stuart Radcliffe **Mawson** 1918-2008

Chaplain: Captain Henry **Irwin**. He was killed on the 22nd. He was 28.

Regimental Sergeant Major: W.O. I F.A. **Bancroft**

Headquarters Company

Commanding Officer: Major Daniel Robert Wyndham **Webber** 1913-1993

Commander Signals Platoon Lt. William George **Fleet**

Administration Officer: 2/Lt. H.I. **McBishop**

Motor Transport Officer: Lt. Laurence **Atkinson** 1919-

RQMS: W.O.II D. **Morris**

Instructor A.P.T.C.: W.O.II A.F. Riches

Company Sergeant Major: (Acting W.O.I) Sergeant Bernard W. **Bartholomew**. He was killed on the 18th at the age of 28.

Support Company

Officer Commanding: Captain Sir Frank Douglas **King** 1919-1998

Second in Command: Captain Peter Hyde **Forshall** 1905-1980

Company Sergeant Major: W.O.II G. **Gatland**, MBE

Commander Mortar Platoon: Lt. Reginald L. **Thomas**. He was killed on the 21st. He was 28.

Second in Command: Lt. James L. **McKenna**. This 26 year old Canloan officer was killed on the 22nd.

Commander MMG Platoon: Lt. James Fraser **Rogerson**. He was killed on the 24th. He was 21.

Commander Assault Platoon: Lt. Frank **Crawford**. He was killed on the 22nd at the age of 32.

A Company

Commanding Officer: Major David Alexander **Gilchrist** 1920-2003

Second in Command: Captain Peter John **Perse** 1916-1990

Company Sergeant Major: W.O.II George W. **Ashdown** MM. He was killed on the 20th. He was 30.

Commander No. 1 Platoon: Lt. Arthur Andrew **Vickers** 1920-

Commander No. 2 Platoon: Lt. William Albert P. **Grose** 1921-1996

Commander No. 3 Platoon: Lt. R. **Wood**

B Company

Officer Commanding: Major: Guy L. **Blacklidge**. He was killed on the 23rd and the 29 year old has no known grave.

Second in Command: Captain John S. **Douglas** He was killed on the 21st at 23.

Company Sergeant Major: W.O.II S. **Smith**

Commander No. 4 Platoon: 2/Lt. Wilfred H. **Speke**. He was killed on the 21st at 30.

Commander No. 5 Platoon: Lt. Anthony Lambert Tennant **Hoyle** 1923-1985

Commander No. 6 Platoon: 2/Lt. James Eric **Blackwood** MC 1915-1976

C Company

Officer Commanding: Major Peter Middleton **Milo** 1919-1986

Second in Command: Captain Edward James **Edwards**

Company Sergeant Major: W.O.II **Brown**

Commander No.7 Platoon: Lt. Richard de Courcy **Peele**. He was killed on the 22nd at 20.

Commander No. 8 Platoon: Lt. Keith Foster **Bell** 1920-2005

Commander No. 9 Platoon: Lt. George Henry **Fitzgerald**

1st Airlanding Brigade

The brigade served in India in 1940 as the 31st Independent Infantry Brigade and became the 1st Airlanding Brigade in November 1941. Brigadier Hicks took command in time for the Sicily Campaign. The brigade headquarters had 12 officers and 68 other ranks at Arnhem and only 3 officers and 18 other ranks returned.

Headquarters

Commanding Officer: Brigadier Philip Hugh Whitby **Hicks**, DSO,MB, CBE 1895-1967

Deputy Commander: Colonel Hilaro N. **Barlow**, OBE He was killed on the 19th. NKG

Brigade Major: Major Charles Anthony Howell Bruce **Blake**, DSC 1911-1951

Intelligence Officer: Lt. William R. **Burns**. He was killed on the 20th at the age of 31.

Deputy Assistant Adjutant Quartermaster: Captain Donald Hotham **Robson** 1908-1981

Staff Captain: Captain Edward A. **Moy-Thomas** He was killed on the 20th at 34.

Brigade RASC Officer: Captain Leslie Arthur George **Lockyer** 1913-1994

Brigade Signals Officers: Captain Stuart L. **Blatch**. He was killed on the 20th at the age of 23.

Lt. John Ellis **Drake**, MC

Liaison Officer: S. Staff.: Lt. George N. **Austin**. He was killed on the 24th at the age of 24.

Liaison Officer: 7 K.O.S.B.: Lt. John **Clark**

Instructor A.P.T.C.: W.O.II Leskie **Morgan**. He was killed on the 24th at the age of 38.

Commander Bde Defence Pl.: Lt. Anthony R. **Thomas**. He was killed on the 20th at age of 25.

Defence Pl. Sergeant Major: W.O.II J. **Jeffries**

Reverend: Bernard J. **Benson**. He died of wounds on the 27th at 30.

2nd (Airborne) Battalion, The South Staffordshire Regiment

It was a regular army battalion in India at the outbreak of the war and suffered heavily in Sicily after it had been converted to a glider borne infantry. Of the total of 46 officers and 736 other ranks that fought at Arnhem, only 6 officers and 134 other ranks returned.

Headquarters

Commanding Officer: Lt-Col. William Derek Hessing **McCardie** 1912-1977

Second in Command: Major John Conway **Commings**, MiD 1913-1997

Adjutant: Captain John Frederick King **Chapman** 1916-1990

Assistant Adjutant: Lt. Ralph Harding **Schwartz** 1916-1990

Intelligence Officer: Lt. David Gordon **Longden** 1915-1997

Medical Officer: Captain Brian **Brownscombe** GM. The 29 year old was murdered on the 24th of September.

Brigade Liaison Officer: Lt. D. **Parker**

Regimental Sergeant Major: W.O.I D. **Slater**

Signals Platoon: Lt. H. **Cartwright**

Headquarters Company

Commanding Officer: Major John Mallor **Simonds**. He died on the 23rd at the age of 29.

Commander Carriers: Lt. Arthur R. **Godfrey** (Canloan)

Company Sergeant Major: W.O.II Frank A.**Bluff** 1915-1979

Commander Signals Platoon: Lt. Hugh Harry Langon **Cartwright** 1920-2004

Commander Pioneer Platoon: Lt. Ernest Frederick **Walters** 1921-1988

Support Company

Commanding Officer: Major John Stewart Aitchison **Buchanan** DSO 1913-1968

Second in Command: Captain Basil William H. **Hingston**. This Canloan officer was killed on the 19th at the age of 29.

Commander Mortar Group: Captain Arthur Hambly **Willcocks** 1918-1986

Commander No.1 Mortar Pl: Lt. Jack **Reynolds**, MC

Commander No.2 Mortar Pl: Lt. Leonard **Withers**, MC

Commander MMG Group: Unknown

Commander No. 1 MMG Pl.: Lt. Charles James **MacDonnell** 1921-90

Commander No. 2 MMG Pl.: Lt. W. Alexander **Harvie**, MiD Canloan

Commander Anti Tank Gp.: Captain Geoffrey Calvin **Woodward** 1913-

Commander No. 1 AT Pl.: Lt. Eric Henry Dunn **Butler** 1918-1994

Commander No. 2 AT Pl.: unknown

A Company

Commanding Officer: Major Thomas Benjamin **Lane**

Second in Command: Captain John Brewster **McCooke** 1915-1992

Company Sergeant Major: W.O.II V. **Williams**

Commander No. 7 Platoon: Lt. William Charles **Withnall** 1918-1976

Commander No. 8 Platoon: Lt. Alan Ernest **Barker** 1923-

Commander No. 9 Platoon: Lt. Robert Anthony **Barrett** 1920-1996

Commander No. 10 Platoon: Lt. Geoffrey William **Glassborow** 1922-2011

B Company

Officer Commanding: Major Robert Henry **Cain** VC 1909-1974

Second in Command: Captain Reginald Sydney **Foot** MC 1913-1960

Company Sergeant Major: W.O.II William **Robinson**, MC

Commander No. 11 Platoon: Lt. James William **Taylor** (Canloan) 1920-2010

Commander No. 12 Platoon: Lt. Georges **Dupenois** 1921-

Commander No. 13 Platoon: Lt. Carlisle **Norwood** (Canloan) unk-2002

Commander No. 14 Platoon: Lt. Roland **Sharp**

Attached: Lt. John James M. **MacDonald**, MM (Canloan) 1919-2008

C Company

Officer Commanding: Major Philip Richard Thomas **Wright**. He was killed on the 19th at the age of 23.

Second in Command: Captain John Raymond **Dickens** 1914-1997

Company Sergeant Major: W.O.II Douglas Aubrey **Godfrey** He died of his wounds on the 28th at the age of 27.

Commander No. 15 Platoon: Lt. Philip Hart **Turner**, DSC Canloan

Commander No. 16 Platoon: Lt. Philip Brandon **Evans**

Commander No. 17 Platoon: Lt. Donald Kenneth **Edwards** MC 1923-1997

Commander No. 18 Platoon: Lt. John **Badger**, MC. He killed in action.

D Company

Officer Commanding: Major John Etherington **Philip** 1919-1988

Second in Command: Captain Ernest Mariel **Wyss** MiD. He was killed on the 19th.

Company Sergeant Major: W.O.II R. **Bowditch**

Commander No.19 Platoon: Lt. Albert E. **Boustead** (Canloan)

Commander No. 20 Platoon: Lt. John Ernest **Hardman-Mountford** 1917-1971

Commander No. 21 Platoon: Lt. Ernest **Roebuck** He was killed on the 19th at the age of 24.

Commander No. 22 Platoon: Lt. James S. **Erskine** (Canloan)

1st (Airborne) Battalion, The Border Regiment

This regular battalion suffered heavily in France in 1940 and in Sicily after it had been converted to glider borne infantry. Replacements came from Lancashire and the North-East. At Arnhem there were 43 officers and 754 other ranks present and only 9 officers and 241 other ranks returned.

Headquarters

Commanding Officer: Lt-Col. Thomas H. **Haddon** 1913-1993

Second in Command: Major Henry Stuart **Cousens** 1914-2004

Adjutant: Captain Colin Martin **Douglas** 1912-1991

Intelligence Officer: Lt. Ronald Christopher **Hope-Jones** 1920-2000

Liaison/ Administration Off: Lt. Douglas Henry **Skilton** MiD 1922-

Medical Officer: Captain John **Graham-Jones**

Chaplain: Captain John J. **Rowell**, MiD

Regimental Sergeant Major: W.O.I Albert **Pope**. He died of his wounds on the 22nd. He was 34.

Sergeant Major: W.O.II James **Smith**

Headquarters Company

Officer Commanding: Major Dennis Richard Lawrence **Morrisey**

Company Sergeant Major: W.O.II Leslie S. **Fielding**, BS

Commander Signals Platoon: Lt. Joseph Stephenson Davidson **Hardy**, MC 1917-2005

Commander Pioneer Platoon: Lt. Alan Harvey **Cox** 1923-

Instructor A.P.T.C. W.O.II Frederick **Connett**

Support Company

Officer Commanding: Major Richard Henry **Stewart** 1916-1993

Second in Command and MMG Group: Captain Thomas Wood Ingram **Cleasby** 1920-2009

Commander 27 MMG Pl.: Lt. Joseph **Tate**. He was killed on the 22nd at the age of 22.

Commander 28 MMG Pl: Lt. John Stewart Granville **McCartney** 1919-1993

Company Sergeant Major: W.O.II Norman **Ursell**

Commander Mortar Group: Captain Barry Barnett **Ingram** MiD 1916-1988

Commander 23 Mortar Pl: Lt. Michael Robert **Holman** BL 1921-1985

Commander 24 Mortar Pl: Lt. George Blain **Coulhard** 1921-1988

Commander AT Group: Captain Robert Miles Anthony **Reese** 1921-

Commander 25 AT Pl.: Lt. John Anthony **Howe** 1911-

Commander 26 AT Pl.: Lt. Edward Selwyn **Newport** 1921-

A Company

Officer Commanding: Major T.E. **Montgomery.** He died of his wounds on the 21st.

Second in Command: Captain Baldwin **Wilson** 1917-2002

Company Sergeant Major: W.O.II Frederick A. **Grimshaw**

Commander No. 7 Platoon: Lt. Patrick **Ballie** 1920-1973

Commander No. 8 Platoon: Lt. Clifford Mervin **Aasen** (Canloan) 1917-1954

Commander No. 9 Platoon: Lt. Robert Hugh **Coulston** He was killed on the 23rd at 24.

Commander No. 10 Platoon: Lt. Edmund Filford **Scrivenr** 1916-2003

B Company

Officer Commanding: Major Thomas Wilfred Welburn **Armstrong** 1914-1991

Second in Command: Lt. William Patrick **Stott** 1922-

Company Sergeant Major: W.O.II Alfred B. **McGladdery**

Commander No. 11 Platoon: Lt. Stanley **Barnes**

Commander No. 12 Platoon: Lt. Arthur Robert **Royall** 1919-

Commander No. 13 Platoon: Lt. John Arthur **Welbelove** (Canloan) He was killed on the 21st at the age of 24.

Commander No. 14 Platoon: Sgt. Thomas **Watson** He was killed on the 21st at the age of 28.

C Company

Officer Commanding: Major William **Neill**, DSO -1984

Second in Command: Captain W. Gordon **Welch**

Company Sergeant Major: W.O.II George Henry **Stringer**

Commander No. 15 Platoon: Lt. Alan Douglas **Roberts**, SS 1917-2005

Commander No. 16 Platoon: Lt. George W. **Comper** (Canloan)

Commander No. 17 Platoon: Lt. Robert Claude **Crittenden**

Commander No. 18 Platoon: Lt. Percy George **Boville** (Canloan)

D Company

Officer Commanding: Major Charles Fred Osbourne **Breese**, DSC 1916-1982

Second in Command: Captain William K. **Hodgson**. He died of his wounds on the 26th at the age of 24.

Company Sergeant Major: W.O.II Herbert **Thyer**

Commander No. 19 Platoon: Lt. Jack Mackenzie **Bainbridge** 1918-

Commander No. 20 Platoon: Lt. Alan Thomas **Green** 1921-2004

Commander No. 21 Platoon: Lt. Philip S. **Holt**. He was killed on the 21st at the age of 19.

Commander No. 22 Platoon: Lt. George E.T. **Brown**. He was killed on the 23rd.

7th (Galloway) Battalion, Kings Own Scottish Borderers (Airborne)

For most of the war this battalion was part of the Orkney and Shetland Defence Force and never fought a battle until it was converted to gliders and landed at Arnhem. Its commanding officer was the only battalion commander not to be killed or captured. Lieutenant-Colonel Payton-Ried and 2 of his officers and 74 other ranks returned, out of a total of 44 officers and 776 other ranks that landed at Arnhem.

Headquarters

Commanding Officer: Lt.-Col. Robert **Payton-Reid**, DSO 1897-1971

Second in Command: Major John Sacheverell A'Deane **Coke**, MiD. He was killed on the 18th.

Adjutant: Captain David **Clayhills** 1919-1998

Intelligence Officer: Lt. Alexander **MacKenzie**

Liaison/Administration Off: Lt. Robert Finlay **Wilson** 1914-2000

Medical Officer: Captain Brian **Devlin** 1919-1997

Chaplain: Captain James Gilbert **Morrison** 1915-2008

Regimental Sergeant Major: W.O. I W.M.C. **Lamb**

Headquarters Company

Officer Commanding: Major Alexander V. **Cochran**. He was killed on the 20th at the age of 31.

Company Sergeant Major: W.O.II O.W. **Drummond**

Commander Signals Pl.: Lt. William James Melville **Lamond**, SS 1916-1985

Commander Pioneer Pl.: Lt. John **Chrystal**

Support Company

Officer Commanding: Major Henry Ralph **Hill**. He was killed on the 18th at the age of 38.

Second in Command: unfilled

Company Sergeant Major: W.O.II L.J. **Stayton**

MMG Group: Captain George Blain **Coulthard** 1921-1988

Commander 1 MMG Pl.: Lt. Alexander Weir **Robertson-Durham**

Commander 2 MMG Pl: Lt. Thomas E. **Donaldson**

Commander Mortar Group: Captain George William **Steer** 1987-

Commander 1 Mortar Pl: Lt. Charles Marius **Pelissier** 1913-

Commander 2 Mortar Pl: Lt. Alexanderer K. **Crighton**. He was killed on the 20th at 26.

Commander AT Group: Captain Ronald **Bannatyne** 1917-

Commander 1 AT Pl.: Lt. Alexander **Hannah**

Commander 2 AT Pl.: Lt. Arthur D.L. **Sharlpes**. He died of his wounds on the 21st at 23.

A Company

Officer Commanding: Major Robert Gilliam **Buchanan**, BL 1908-1985

Second in Command: Captain James Frederik **McCourt** (Canloan) ?-2004

Company Sergeant Major: W.O.II W. **Henderson**

Commander No. 1 Platoon: Lt. Lawrence **Kane** (Canloan)

Commander No. 2 Platoon: Lt. George Smith **MacDonald** (Canloan) 1918-2008

Commander No. 3 Platoon: Lt. Donald Arthur **Cameron** (Canloan)

Commander No. 4 Platoon: Lt. James H. **Strang**. He was killed on the 19th at the age of 28.

B Company

Officer Commanding: Major Michael Bertram **Forman** 1921-2005

Second in Command: Captain James S. **Dundas**. He was killed on the 25th.

Company Sergeant Major: W.O.II F. **Bodle**

Commander No. 5 Platoon: Lt. Alexander D.M. **Murray**. He was killed on the 18th at 19.

Commander No. 6 Platoon: Lt. Edward Robert Erskine **Carter** (Canloan) 1923-1982

Commander No. 7 Platoon: Lt. Charles **Doig** 1914-2007

Commander No. 8 Platoon: Lt. Cyril John **Ashley** 1914-2011

C Company

Officer Commanding: Major Gordon Maitland **Dinwiddle** 1916-1998

Second in Command: Captain James Stewart **Livingstone**, MC

Company Sergeant Major: W.O.II W. **Buchanan**

Commander No. 9 Platoon: Lt. Alan R. **Hunter**. He was killed on the 20th.

Commander No. 10 Platoon: Lt. Albert E.F. **Wayte** (Canloan). He died on the 20th at 27.

Commander No. 11 Platoon: Lt. Martin L. **Kaufmann** (Canloan) 1919-

Commander No. 12 Platoon: Lt. James William **Taylor** (Canloan) 1920-2010

D Company

Officer Commanding: Major Charles Gordon **Sheriff**, DSO 1916-2003

Second in Command: Captain George Cleland **Gourlay** 1913-1999

Company Sergeant Major: W.O.II J. **Swanston**, MiD

Commander No. 13 Platoon: Lt. Joseph Maclean **Hunter**. He was killed on the 21 at the age of 24.

Commander No. 14 Platoon: Lt. William Glyndwr **Beddoe** 1919-

Commander No. 15 Platoon: Lt. Albert E. **Kipping** (Canloan). He was killed on the 18th at 21.

Commander No. 16 Platoon: Lt. Peter Brown **Mason** (Canloan) 1921-

Divisional Troops:

1st Airborne Reconnaissance Squadron

This unit formed at the same time as the division came into being. It was equipped with jeeps and motorcycles. The majority of the 25 officers and 181 other ranks landed by parachute. Only 9 officers and 66 men returned.

Headquarters

Commanding Officer: Major Charles Frederick Howard 'Freddie' **Gough**, MC MiD 1901-1977

Second in Command: Captain David **Allsop**, BL 1917-1987

Adjutant: Captain James Geoffrey **Costeloe**, MiD 1920-2009

Intelligence Officer: Lt. Trevor V.R. **McNabb**. He was shot during an escape attempt. He was 22.

Liaison Officer: Lt. Alexander A. **Lickerish**

Signals Officer: Lt. Frederick W. **Ladds**, MiD

Quartermaster: Lt. Tom **Collier** 1913-1987

Medical Officer: Captain Thomas Douglas Victor **Swinscow**, BC 1917-1992

Squadron Sergeant Major: W.O.II G.C. **Meadows**

QM. Sergeant Major: W.O.II George E. **Holderness**, MiD He was killed on the 25th at 30.

Special Liaison to HQ: Captain Harry **Poole**

Headquarters Troop

Commanding Officer: Captain Horace A. **Platt**. He was shot on the 23rd during an escape attempt. He was 30 years old.

Lt. John Graham Hilton **Wadsworth**, BS 1924-

Lt. Herbert E. **Pearson**, MC. He was killed on the 19th at 23.

Support Troop

Commanding Officer: Lt. John A. **Christie**. He was killed on the 20th at 23.

A Troop

Commanding Officer: Captain Michael Wathing **Grubb** 1920-1993

Commander No. 1 Section: Lt. John **Stevenson**

Commander No. 2 Section: Lt. Doug **Galbraith**, MiD, MC

Commander No. 3 Section: Lt. David Robert **Guthrie** 1922-2003

* note: B Troop was lost in Italy and never reconstituted.

C Troop

Commanding Officer: Captain John Arthur **Hay** 1912-

Commander No. 7 Section: Lt. Ralph Colwyn **Foulkes** 1922-

Commander No. 8 Section: Lt. Peter L. **Bucknall**. He was killed on the 17th at 23.

Commander No. 9 Section: Lt. Cecil **Bretingham** Bowles 1924-2009

D Troop

Commanding Officer: Captain John R.C.R. **Park**. He was killed on the 24th.

Commander No. 10 Section: Lt. John Wilson **Marshall**, MiD

Commander No. 11 Section: Lt. William F.V. **Hodge**.

Commander No. 12 Section: Lt. Alan F. **Pascal**. He was killed on the 24. He was 20.

21st Independent Parachute Company

Formed in 1942 there were about a couple dozen anti-Nazi German and Austrian refugees who changed their names to hide their roots in their ranks. The company's role was to act as pathfinders for the division. It was to land ahead of the main force and set-up visual and electronic navigational aids on the correct drop and landing zones. Of the 6 officers and 186 other ranks, 5 officers and 108 men returned.

Commanding Officer:	Major Bernard Alexander `Boy' **Wilson**, MC, MiD, DSO 1897-1965
Second in Command:	Captain Robert Edward **Spivey** MiD 1921-1994
Intelligence Officer:	Lt. John **Horsley**. He died of his wounds on the 27th at 24.
Company Sergeant Major:	W.O.II J. **Steward**, DCM
Commander No. 1 Platoon:	Lt. Herbert David **Eastwood** MC 1919-2010
Commander No. 2 Platoon:	Lt. Cecil Edmund Kirby **Speller** 1924-2008
Commander No. 3 Platoon:	Lt. Norman Hugh Harry **Ashmore**, MC 1922-

1st Airborne Ordnance Field Park Company

Went in: 3 officers and 25 other ranks. None returned.

Assistant Director of Ordnance Services: Lt-Col. Gerald Hubrey **Mobbs** 1911-1976

Advanced Para. Recce Party: Captain Bernard Vincent **Manley** 1910-2005

Second in Command: Captain Cecil Cyril **Chidgey** 1912-2004

Senior Technical Clerk HQ 1 Airborne Division: W.O.I G.E. **Jenkins**

Ordnance W.O. 1st A/L Bde: W.O.I F.F. **Eastwood**

Ordnance W.O. 4th Para. Bde: W.O.I E. **Higham**

Ordnance W.O. 1st Para. Bde: W.O.I L.N. **Halsall**

Royal Regiment of Artillery

Its purpose was to provide fire support for the 3 brigades and to provide links to outside artillery units when they came into range. Of the 7 officers and 10 other ranks that made up the headquarters, 5 officers and 1 man returned.

Headquarters

Commander Royal Artillery: Lieutenant-Colonel Robert Guy **Loder-Symonds** DSO, DSC 1913-1945

Brigade Major: Major Philip Thomas **Tower**, MBE 1917-2006

Intelligence Officer: Lt. Charles Hilary **Barber** 1922-2002

Staff Lieutenant: Lt. Patrick Rupert Richard **de Burgh**, MiD 1923-2010

E & M Engineers Officer: Captain Ronald Lionel **Hayward** 1914-2000

Signals Officer: 2/Lt. George Christopher **Marshall**. He was killed on the 26th.

Medical Officer: Lt. Derek Henry **Randall** 1921-

Commander F.O.U. Signals: Captain Christopher Woodroffe **Ikin** 1921-1998

1st Airlanding Light Regiment, RA

It formed in February 1943 with American made 75mm guns that could easily fit into a glider. It saw action in Italy. Of the 36 officers and 336 other ranks that landed at Arnhem, 15 officers and 141 other ranks returned.

Headquarters

Commanding Officer: Lt-Col. William Francis Kynaston `Sheriff' **Thompson** MBE BL 1909-1980

Second in Command: Major G.F. **de Gex**, DSC

Adjutant: Lt. Alan Peters **Humphries**

Survey Officer: Lt. Roderick Percy **Pearson** 1921-2007

Signals Officer: Lt. Robert A. **Gregg**. He was killed on the 26th.

Intelligence Officer: Lt. Richard **Corben** 1920-1995

Medical Officer: Captain Victor David Randall **Martin** MiD 1919-2001

Chaplain: Captain Selwyn **Thorne** 1914-

Regimental Sergeant Major: W.O.I J.S. **Siely** OBE

Attached from 112 Fd. Regt.: Captain T. **Rose**. He was killed on the 25th.

Captain A. **Trotman**

1st Airlanding Light Battery, R.A.

Headquarters

Battery Commander: Major Arthur Fairfax **Norman-Walker**. He was killed on the 22nd at the age of 32.

Battery Captain: Captain John Burley **Dickinson**

Command Post Officer: Lt. Christopher Winthrop **Fogarty** 1921-2005

Assistant CPO: Lt. Donald Cecil Clifford **Siggins** 1917-

Battery Sergeant Major: W.O.II A.J. **Jemmet**

A Troop

Troop Commander: Captain John Henry Dixon **Lee** 1919-1997

Gun Position Officer: Lt. Thomas Robert **Barron** 1918-2001

Troop Leader: Lt. Roy Glinn **Staddon** 1921-2014

Troop Sergeant Major: Sgt. A.E. **Reed**

B Troop

Troop Commander: John Waine **Walker**, MiD 1922-2011

Gun Position Officer: Lt. Ian O. **Meikle**. He was killed on the 21st at the age of 24.

Troop Leader: Lt. Keith C. **Halliday**. He was killed on the 23rd.

Troop Sergeant Major: W.O.II R.S. **Barrett** MM

2nd (Oban) Airlanding Light Battery, R.A.

Headquarters

Battery Commander: Major James Edward Fryer **Linton** DSO 1909-1989

Battery Captain: Captain Basil Anthony Bethune **Taylor**, SS 1918-2000

Command Post Officer: Lt. Carmel S. **Leitch**. He was killed on the 24th at the age of 21.

Assistant CPO: Lt. R. **Corben**

Battery Sergeant Major: W.O.II W.A. **Goodman**

C Troop

Troop Commander: Captain Peter **Chard**, MiD. He died of his wounds on October 9th, 1944 at the age of 24.

Gun Position Officer: Lt. Adrian **Donaldson** DSO 1922-

Troop Leader: Lt. Kenneth Grayston **White** 1917-2009

Troop Sergeant Major: W.O.II T.E.V **Morgan**, MiD

D Troop

Troop Commander: Captain Percy Albert **Taylor**. He was killed on the 24th at the age of 31.

Gun Position Officer: Lt. James H. **Woods**. He was killed on the 25th at the age of 28.

Troop Leader: unfilled

Troop Sergeant Major: W.O.II J. **Jubb**

3rd Airlanding Light Battery, R.A.

Headquarters

Battery Commander: Major Dennis Stewart **Munford**, BL 1912-2002

Battery Captain: Captain David **Lindsay**

Command Post Officer: Lt. Peter William **Wilkinson**, MC 1922-

Assistant C.P.O.: Lt. John Wicks **Widdicombe** 1918-2005

Battery Sergeant Major: W.O.II A. **Garnett**

E Troop

Troop Commander: Captain Charles Anthony **Harrison**, MC 1918-1995

Gun Position Officer: Lt. Noel Frank **Farrands** 1919-

Troop Leader: Lt. (Sir) Anthony Victor **Driver** 1920-2002

Troop Sergeant Major: W.O.II David **Lawson**. He was killed either on the 19th or 20th at the age of 31.

F Troop

Troop Commander: Captain Tudor Morgan **Griffiths** 1921-

Gun Position Officer: Lt. Thomas Allen **Conlin** 1914-1991

Troop Leader: Lt. Francis Pepys Durie **Moore** 1924-2014

Troop Sergeant Major: W.O.II T.W. **Kent**

1st Airlanding Anti Tank Battery

Formed from a pre-war Territorial Army unit in Barrow-in-Furness to provide the division with AT weapons. A total of 26 6-pounder and 8 17-pounder anti-tank guns would arrive at Arnhem. Of the 14 officers and 167 other ranks, only 2 officers and 60 other ranks returned from Arnhem.

Headquarters

Battery Commander: Major William Frank **Arnold** 1908-1997

Battery Captain `G': Captain N. **McLeod**

Battery Captain `Q': Captain Henry Fairbrother **Bear**
ₐ 1914-1995

Liaison Officers: Lt. J.A. **Cox**

Lt. Harry **Whittaker**. He was killed on the 20th at the age of 28.

Lt. Geoffrey **Ryall**

Battery Sergeant Major: W.O.II **L. Doughty**

Commander A Troop: Lt. Edward Eric **Clapham**, MC 1922-1989

Lt. B.S. **Lockett**

Commander B Troop: Lt. P. **McFarlane**

Commander C Troop: Lt. Edward Ernest **Shaw**, MC 1918-2005

Commander D Troop: LT John Thomas **Lewis** 1914-1981

Commander P Troop: Lt. Thomas **Casey**

Commander Z Troop: Lt. Eustace Arthur **McNaught** 1922-1992

2nd Airlanding Anti Tank Battery, R.A.

This battery formed from a pre-war Territorial Army unit in Oban. On route to Italy the ship that the battery was on hit a mine and the battery suffered heavily. Reinforcements were made up from 'volunteers'* in North Africa. It had 26 6-pounders and 8 17-pounders. Only 1 officer and 56 other ranks of the 11 officers and 162 other ranks returned. (*only 1 man volunteered, the other 50 were volun-told).

Headquarters

Battery Commander: Major Aannesley Freeman **Haynes** 1909-1999

Battery Captain 'A': Captain Peter Roderik McGregor **Barron**, MiD. He was killed on the 26th at 22 years of age.

Batter Captain 'Q': Captain James Roland **Elliott** 1916-1985

Liaison Officers: Lt. W. **McInnes**

Lt. Eric **Withecombe** 1920-2005

Lt. Cyril **Palmer**. He was killed on the 19th.

Battery Sergeant Major: W.O.II H.J. **Baxter**. He was killed on the 20th at the age of 32.

Commander E Troop: Lt. Robert G. **Glover**, MiD. He was killed on the 19th at the age of 25.

Commander F Troop: Lt. Robert L. **McLaren**. He was killed on the 18th at the age of 30.

Commander G Troop: Lt. Leslie Owen **Harding** 1913-1984

Commander H Troop: Lt. Frederick William **Ellis**

Commander X Troop: Lt. George Arthur **Paull** 1909-1993

No. 1 Forward Observer Unit R.A. (Airborne)

The Forward Observation Officers (FOOs) acted with the divisional artillery and, if available, coordinated with outside artillery to provide fire support intelligence. These men came from a pool of volunteers so they have no regional character. A total of 17 officers and 91 other ranks landed at Arnhem and 8 officers and 36 other ranks returned.

Attached to Divisional HQ:

Commanding Officer: Captain Arthur Edgar **O'Grady** 1915-1994

Attached to 1st Para. Brigade:

Brigade Headquarters: Captain Colin Osboure **Kennedy** 1921-1984 (was not at Arnhem)

1st Parachute Battalion: Captain William Small **Caird** 1917-1987

2nd Parachute Battalion: Captain Henry S. **Buchanan**. He was killed on the 19th at 30.

3rd Parachute Battalion: Captain Dudley C.O. **Bowerman** He died of his wounds on the 19th at the age of 24.

Attached to 4th Para. Brigade:

Brigade Headquarters: Captain E.I. **Gilman**

Captain Thomas Visger **Miller** 1921-1997

156 Parachute Battalion: Captain Raymond H. **Stevens**. He died on the 24th at 26.

10 Parachute Battalion: Captain William Swanson **Whimister**, MiD 1910-1992

11 Parachute Battalion: Captain John Lloyd **Brown**

Attached to 1st Airlanding Brigade:

Brigade Headquarters: Captain Christopher John S. **McMillen**, BC 1916-1989

1st Bn, The Border Regiment: Captain Stanley Benjamin **Birchmore** 1920-1995

2nd Bn., South Staff. Regt.: Captain Roderick G.A. **Gow**. He was killed on the 19th at 21.

7th Bn., K.O.S.B. Regt.: Captain John Adair **Langford**

Attached to Divisional Troops:

Headquarters R.A.: Captain Christopher Woodroffe **Ikin** 1921-1998

1st Airborne Recce Sqn.: Captain William John **Mallet**

Attached to XXX Corps:

Commanding Officer: Major R.D. **Wight-Boycott**

Second in Command: Captain M.W. **Braithwaite**

Officers: Lt. G.W. **Davey**

Lt. C.M. **Hewat**

Lt. J.L. **Meish**

Corps of Royal Engineers

The purpose of this group was to provide engineering support to the division. This meant everything from demolitions to clearing mines to building bridges, though the bridging equipment wasn't to be provided until later.

Headquarters had 4 officers and 13 other ranks at Arnhem and 3 officers and 9 other ranks returned.

The **1st Parachute Squadron** had 10 officers and 132 other ranks land and 3 officers and 13 other ranks returned.

The **4th Parachute Squadron** had 10 officers and 135 other ranks land and 5 officers and 64 other ranks returned.

The **9th Field Company** had 8 officers and 194 other ranks land and 1 officer and 79 other rank returned.

The **261st Field Park Company** had 1 officer and 22 other ranks land and 8 other ranks returned.

Headquarters

Commanding Officer: Lt-Col. Edmund Charles Wolf `Eddie' **Myers** CBE DSO BL 1906-1997

Adjutant: Captain Michael Douglas **Green** BS 1920-

Intelligence Officer: Lt. Crofton Edmund Peter **Sankey** He was killed on the 23rd at 21.

Field Engineer: Lt. David Valentine **Storrs** MC 1923-1956

1st Parachute Squadron, R.E.

Commanding Officer: Major Douglas Campbell **Murray** MC 1913-2005

Second in Command: Captain Stephen **George**, MC

Intelligence Officer: Lt. Donald Rostron **Hindley** MiD 1919-

Squadron Sergeant Major: W.O.II J. **Ellis**

Commander A Troop: Captain Eric MacLachlan **Mackay**, MBE DSC 1921-1995

Lt. Richard A. **Robertson**. He was killed on the 21st.

Commander B Troop: Captain Trevor John **Livesey** MC 1920-1959

Lt. Denis Jackson **Simpson**, MC, MiD 1921-1989

Lt. Peter **Stainforth**

Commander C Troop: Captain Cecil Gordon **Cox** 1922-2005

Lt. Robert Holland **Walpole**

4th Parachute Squadron, R.E.

Commanding Officer: Major Aeneas John Martin **Perkins**, MiD 1918-1996

Second in Command: Captain Nigel Beaumont **Thomas**, MC MiD. He was killed on the 20th at 28.

Intelligence Officer: Lt. George Samuel **Harris** 1923-1999

Squadron Sergeant Major: W.O.II E.S.J. **Marriott**

Commander No. 1 Troop: Captain James Gordon Anstruther **Smith** 1920-

Lt. Kenneth Charles **Evans** 1922-2000

Commander No. 2 Troop: Captain J.J. **McCormie**

Lt. Michael C. **Eden**. He was killed on the 21st at 22.

Commander No. 3 Troop: Captain Harry **Faulkner-Brown** MC 1920-2008

Lt. Norman Leslie B. **Thomas**
1916-

2/Lt. Kenneth Arthur **Hall**

9th Field Company (Airborne) Company, R.E.

Commanding Officer: Major John Chisholm **Winchester**
MC 1912-1992

Second in Command: Captain Peter Hindley **Wetherill**
1919-1909

Intelligence Officer: Lt. Edgar Gerald **Wise** 1921-1999

Company Sergeant Major: W.O.II **Cousins**

Commander No. 1 Platoon: Captain Roger B. **Binyon**
He was killed on the 24th at 30.

Commander No. 2 Platoon: Captain E.C. **O'Callaghan**
MC MiD

Lt. Roy E.J.W. **Timmins**
He was killed on the 17th at 23.

Commander No. 3 Platoon: Captain Maurice **Heggie**
1920-1923

Lt. James **Steel**

261st Field Park Company, R.E.

Commander Detachments: Lt. William Henderson **Skinner**
He was murdered as a POW on the
20th at the age of 24.

Royal Army Service Corps

This group was responsible for the collection and dispersal of supplies. Only a small portion of the division's RASC personnel landed at Arnhem. The bulk were with the Seaborne Tail.

Headquarters 3 officers and 9 other ranks land and 2 officers and 7 other ranks returned.

The **250 Light Composite Company** had 6 officers and 230 other ranks land and 4 officers and 68 other ranks returned.

The **93 Light Composite Company** had 10 other ranks land and 6 of them returned.

Headquarters

Commanding Officer:	Lt-Col. Michael **St. John Packe**, BC 1916-1978
Second in Command:	Major David Graham **Clark** 1919-
Adjutant:	Captain John Denis **Naylor** 1916-1983
	Captain **Winter-Goodwin**

250 (Airborne) Light Composite Company

Commander No. 1 Para. Pl. and 1st Para Jeep Section (1st Para. Bde.)	Captain John Launcelot **Cranmer-Byng** MC 1919-1999
	Lt. John Derek **Grice** MiD 1915-2004
Commander No. 2 Para. Pl & 2nd Para Jeep Section (4th Para. Bde.)	Captain Desmond T. **Kavanagh** He was killed on the 19th at 25.
	Lt. G. **Osbourne**
Commander No. 3 Para. Pl. & 3rd Para. Jeep Section (1st Airlanding Bde.)	Capt. William Vincent Aloysius **Gell** 1920-2005
	2/Lt. L.E.D. **Daniells**
Company Sergeant Major:	W.O.II W. **Gibbs**

1st Airborne Divisional Signals

The division's signal group was responsible for the transmission and receipt of communications within the division and with outside units. A total of 19 officers and 348 other ranks landed at Arnhem and 8 officers and 104 other ranks returned.

Headquarters

Commanding Officer:	Lt-Col. Thomas Godfrey Vaughan **Stephenson**, OBE 1912-1988
Second in Command:	Major Anthony John **Deane-Drummond**, MC, MiD 1917-2012
Adjutant:	Captain Lewis Lawrence **Golden** 1922-
Regimental Sergeant Major:	W.O.I W. **Potesta**

No. 1 Company Divisional Headquarters Signals

Commanding Officer:	Major G.W. **Holbrooke** (not at Arnhem)
A Section Wireless:	Captain John Raymond **Smith**
	Lt. Robert **Hodges**
	Lt. Peter Thorp **Robson** 1920-1984
Commander C Section Lines:	Lt. David Arthur **Polley** 1923-1984
Security Officer:	Captain Maurice Richard **Hewitt** 1921-
Cipher Officer:	Captain Gerad Edmund **Hemelryk** 1917-1947

No 2 Company Brigade and Artillery Signals

Commander J Section 1 Bde: Captain Wilfred James **Marquand**

Lt. John Brown **Cairns** 1923-

Commander K Section 4 Bde: Captain Alan Bishop **Kennett** 1920-

Lt. Richard William **Boshworth** 1920-

Commander L Section 1AL: Captain Staurt L. **Blatch**
He went missing on the 20th at the age of 23.

Lt. John Ellis **Drake**

Commander E Section RA: Lt. Robert A. **Gregg**
He was killed on the 26th at 21.

Co. F Section HQ RA: 2/Lt. George Christopher **Marshall**

Company Sergeant Major: W.O.II F.H. **Clift**

Royal Army Medical Corps

No. 16 Parachute Field Ambulance claim to be the first 'paramedics' and were attached to the 1 Parachute Brigade. All of the unit's 10 officers and 135 other ranks were either killed or captured.

No. 133 Parachute Field Ambulance was a pre-war Croydon Territorial Army unit that was attached to the 4th Parachute Brigade. Only one other rank returned from a total of 10 officers and 129 other ranks that went in.

No. 181 Parachute Field Ambulance was a Croydon Territorial Army unit that was attached to the 1st Airlanding Brigade. Ten other ranks returned out of 10 officers and 126 other ranks that landed at Arnhem.

Headquarters

Ass. Dir. of Medical Services:	Col. Graeme Matthaw **Warrack** OBE, DSO 1913-1985
Dep. Ass. Dir. of Medical S.:	Major Joseph Esmond **Miller** MC 1914-1990
Chaplains:	Captain Daniel **McGowan** MC 1913-1981
	Captain Bernard Joseph **Benson** He died of his wounds on the 27th at the age of 30.

No. 16 Parachute Field Ambulance

Commanding Officer:	Lt-Col. Eric **Townsend**, MC, MiD
Second in Command:	Major Ronald Rodger **Gordon** MC 1914-2003
Specialist Surgeon:	Major Cedric James **Longland** MC, BC 1914-1991
General Duties Surgeon:	Captain Alexander William **Lipmann-Kessel**, MBE, MC 1914-1986
Section 1st Para. Bde. HQ:	Captain Charles Edward C. **Wells** 1917-1993
Section 1st Para. Bn.	Captain Stanley Laurie **Kaye** 1919-2008
Section 2nd Para. Bn.	Captain John James Walton **Tobin** 1919-2007
Section 3rd Para. Bn.	Captain John H. **Keesey** He was killed on November 2nd, 1944 at the age of 28.
Dentist/Anaesthetist:	Captain D.H. **Ridler**, MC, MiD
Anaesthetist:	Lt. Peter Sewell **Allenby** 1918-1971
Regimental Sergeant Major:	W.O.I E.W. **Brock**
Sergeant Major:	W.O.II E.E. **Pruden**

No. 133 Parachute Field Ambulance

Commanding Officer: Lt-Col. William Carson **Alford** OBE MiD 1993-1990

Second in Command: Major Thomas Richard Brian **Courtney** 1911-2001

Specialist Surgeon: Major Peter **Smith** 1916-1995

General Duties Surgeon: Captain William Ian Stuart **Huddleston** 1911-1993

Section J: Captain John **Lawson**, MiD

Section R: Captain Theodore Francis **Redman** 1916-2004

Section: Lt. Donald Edwin **Olliff** 1919-2001

Section L: Captain Anthony Seymour **Barling** 1919-2002

Dentist/Anaesthetist: Captain A.S. **Flockhart**

Anaesthetist: Lt. C.B. **Novel**

Regimental Sergeant Major: W.O.I I. R. **Bowe**

Quarter-master Sergeant: W.O.II P.E. **Gavin**

HQ Airborne Corps: Captain Percy **Louis**
He was killed on the 24th at 29.

No. 181 Parachute Field Ambulance

Commanding Officer: Lt-Col. Arthur Trevor **Marrable** DSO 1909-1954

Second in Command: Major Simon Macleod **Frazer** 1906-1991

Specialist Surgeon: Lt. John **Tiernan**, MBE

General Duties Surgeon: Major Guy **Rigby-Jones** MC 1911-2002

Section Officer: Captain Clifford Alan **Simmons** MiD 1914-2010

Section Officer: Captain John Cuthill **Taylor** 1916-1995

Reverse Section Officer: Captain James T. **Doyle** He was killed on the 21st at 24.

Dentist/Anaesthetist: Captain Peter **Griffin**   -1979

Anaesthetist: Captain George Barton Douglas **Scott** 1918-1992

Resuscitation: Lt. Bruce Carstairs **Jeffry** 1919-1946

Regimental Sergeant Major: W.O.I L.H. **Bryson**, BL

Sergeant Major: W.O.II J. **Atlee**

Attached RAMC

1st Parachute Brigade

Brigade Headquarters: Captain David **Wright**
MC, BL 1917-2011

1st Parachute Battalion: Captain Arthur **Percival**
MiD 1916-200

2nd Parachute Battalion: Captain James Watt **Logan**
DSO, BL

3rd Parachute Battalion: Captain John **Rutherford**
MC, SS 1915-1998

4th Parachute Brigade

Brigade Headquarters: Captain Richard Erskine
Bonham-Carter 1910-1994

156st Parachute Battalion: Captain John Edward **Buck**
1915-06

10th Parachute Battalion: Captain Gareth F.H. **Drayson**
MiD. He was killed on the 19th at 27
years of age.

11th Parachute Battalion: Captain Stuart Radcliffe **Mawson**
1918-1908

1st Airlanding Brigade

Brigade Headquarters: unfilled

1st Bn the Border Regt.: Captain John Graham **Jones**
1917-2005

2nd Bn. South Staff. Regt.: Captain Brian **Brownscombe**
GM. He was murdered on the 24th
at 29.

7th Bn. K.O.S.B. Regt.: Captain Brian **Devlin**
1919-1997

Divisional Troops:

Reconnaissance Squadron: Captain Thomas Douglas Victor **Swinscow**, BC 1917-1992

Light Regiment RA: Captain Victor David Randall **Martin**, MiD 1919-2001

Headquarters RA: Lt. Derrick Henry **Randall** 1921-

Attached to the division:

No. 163 Field Ambulance

Commanding Officer: Lt-Col. Martin Edward Menkin **Herford**, MBE, MC, DSO 1909-

1st Airborne Divisional Workshops REME

The Royal Electrical and Mechanical Engineers (REME) of the division were responsible for the maintenance and repair of everything from small arms to vehicles. Only an Advanced Workshop Detachment (AWD) landed at Arnhem to carry out limited repairs. The main force was with the Seaborne Tail, which carried the bulk of the stores and recovery vehicles. The detachment that landed at Arnhem was 5 officers and 68 other ranks, of which 3 officers and 27 other ranks returned.

Commander REME: Captain Alfred Francis **Ewens** 1909-

Advanced Workshop Detachment

Commander AWD: Lt. Geoffrey **Manning**

Second in Command: Lt. Harry R. **Roberts**

Artificer Sergeant Major: W.O.I Matty **Reed**

Artificer QMSM: W.O.II Ronald A. **Turner**

1st Para. Bde. LAD: W.O.I H. Jaspar **Jaboor**

Artificer Sergeant Major: unfilled

4th Para. Bde LAD:

HQ R.A. Electrical Mechanical Engineer: Lt. Archibald May **Brodie** 1919-

Captain Ronald L. **Hayward** 1914-2000

Abbreviations:

A&Q	Adjutant and Quartermaster
Ass.	Assistant
APTC	Army Physical Training Corps
AT	Anti-tank
BC	Bronze Cross—Netherlands
Bde.	Brigade
BEM	British Empire Medal
BL	Bronze Lion—Netherlands
BK	Bronze Cross-Netherlands
Capt.	Captain
Col.	Colonel
CPO	Commander Post Office
Dir	Director
Div	Division
DCM	Distinguished Conduct Medal
DSC	Distinguished Service Cross-USA
DSO	Distinguished Service
GM	George Medal
HQ	Headquarters
LAD	Light Aid Detachment
Lt.	Lieutenant
MBE	Member of the Most Excellent Order of the British Empire
MC	Military Cross
MG	Machine Gun
MiD	Mentioned in despatches
MMG	Medium Machine Gun
NKG	No known grave.
OBE	Order of the British Empire
Para.	Parachute
QM	Quartermaster
PL	Platoon
R.A.	Royal Artillery
RQMS	Regimental Quartermaster Sergeant
SS	Silver Star (USA)
W.O.	Warrant Officer

Sources:

`Arnhem: The Airborne Battle'* by Martin Middlebrook

`Arnhem the Fight to Sustain: the Untold Story of Airborne Logistics'* by Frank Steer

`British Army of WW2 War Establishment Tables'* by Gary Kennedy

`Codeword Canloan'* by Wilfred I. Smith

`From D-day to VE-day Vol. 2 The British Soldier'* by Jean Bouchey

`Reconstitution of the British Airborne Division'* by Philip Reinders

`Remember Arnhem'* by John Fairley

`Roll of Honour'*, 5th Edition

`The Gunners at Arnhem'* by Peter Wilkinson, MC

`The Holland Patch'* by Simon Haines

`When Dragoons Flew'* by Stuart Eastwood, Charles Gray and Alan Green.

`Who was Who During the Battle of Arnhem'* by C. van Roekel

`With Spanners Descending'* by Joe Roberts

`World War II Unit History officers'* by J.N. (Hans) Houterman

Index

Aitchison; 28
Buchanan, Major Robert Gilliam; 37
Buchanan, W.O.II W.; 38
Buck, Captain John Edward; 17, 62
Bucknall, Lt. Peter L.; 40
Bune, Major John Cuthbert; 7
Burgess, Lt. William D.A.; 22
Burgh, Lt. Patrick Rupert Richard de; 43
Burns, Lt. William; 26
Burwash Lt. B.H.D.; 13
Bush, Major Alan; 13
Bush Lt. Thomas Graham; 17
Bussell, Lt. Raymond M.; 14
Butler, Lt. Eric Henry Dunn; 28
Butterworth, Lt. Alfred David; 3
Byng-Maddick, Major Cecil Distin; 6

Cain, Major Robert Henry; 29
Caird, Captain William Small; 50
Cairns, Lt. John Brown; 6, 57
Cambier, Lt. Harry M.A.; 18
Cameron, Lt. Donald Arthur; 37
Cane, Lt. Peter H.; 2
Carr, Lt. Brian Dean; 21
Carter, Lt. Edward Robert Erskine; 37
Cartwright, Lt. H.; 27
Cartwright, Lt. Hugh Harry Langon; 27
Casey, Lt. Thomas; 48
Chapman, Captain John Frederick King; 27
Chard, Captain Peter; 46
Chenery, W.O.II Ronald McCardie Martin; 18
Chidgey, Captain Cecil Cyril; 42
Christie, Lt. John A.; 40
Chrystal, Lt. John; 36
Clapham, Lt. Edward Eric; 48
Clark, Major David Graham; 55
Clark, Lt. John; 26
Clarke, Lt. John; 21
Clarkson, Lieutenant Alastair Duncan; 7
Clayhills, Captain David; 35
Cleasby, Captain Thomas Wood Ingram; 32
Clegg , Captain Benjamin Beattie; 22
Clegg, Captain James Bianco; 18
Cleminson, Lt. Sir James Arnold Stacey; 14
Clift, W.O.II F.H.; 57

Cochran, Major Alexander V.; 36
Collier, Lt. Tom; 39
Coke, Major John Sacheverell A'Deane; 35
Commings, Major John Conway; 27
Comper, Lt. George W.; 34
Conlin, Lt. Thomas Allen; 47
Connett, W.O.II Frederick; 32
Corben, Lt. R.; 46
Corben, Lt. Richard; 44
Costeloe, Captain James Geoffrey; 39
Coulhard, Lt. George Blain; 36
Coulthard, Captain George Blain; 32
Coulston, Lt. Robert Hugh; 33
Cousens, Major Henry Stuart; 31
Courtie, W.O.II T.J.E.; 22
Courtney, Major Thomas Richard Brian; 60
Cousins, W.O.II; 54
Cox, Lt. Alan Harvey; 31
Cox, Captain Cecil Gordon; 53
Cox, Lt. J.A.; 48
Cranmer-Byng, Captain John Launcelot; 55
Crawford, Lt. Frank; 24
Crawford, Lt. William Patrick Cullen; 23
Crawley, Major Douglas Edward; 11
Crighton, Lt. Alexanderer K.; 36
Crittenden, Lt. Robert; 34
Curtiss, Lieutenant Leslie Arthur; 7

Daniells, 2/Lt. L.E.D.; 55
Davies, Lieutenant Eric J.; 9
Davies, Captain John Alan Emlyn; 8
Davison, Lt. John; 19
Dawson, Major Charles N.B.; 16
Davey, Lt. G.W.; 51
Day, W.O.II A.; 15
Dean, Lieutenant Henry Stanley; 6
Deane Drummond, Major Anthony John; 56
Delacour, Lt. Lindsay D.; 19
Dennison, Major Mervyn William; 14
Deuchar, Captain Ernest; 3, 4
Devlin, Captain Brian; 35, 62
Dickens, Captain John Raymond; 13
Dickson, Lt. Milton Jon Patrick Stanley; 45
Dickinson, Captain John Burley; 45
Dinwiddle, Major Gordon Maitland; 38
Dobie, Lt-Col. David Theodor; 7

Dodd, Lt. Roy G. W.; 21
Doig, Lt. Charles; 37
Donaldson, Lt. Adrian; 46
Donaldson, Lt. Thomas E.; 36
Donaldson, Lt. William S.; 19
Dorrien-Smith, Captain Geoffrey R; 14
Doughty, W.O.II L.; 48
Douglas, Captain Colin Martin; 31
Douglas, Lt. Donald Marsh; 10
Douglas, Captain John S.; 25
Dover, Major Victor; 12
Doyle, Captain James T.; 61
Drake, Lt. John Ellis; 26, 57
Drayson, Captain Gareth F.H.; 20, 62
Driver, Lt. (Sir) Anthony Victor; 47
Drummond, W.O.II O.W.; 36
Dundas, Captain James S.; 37
Dupenois, Lt. Georges; 29

Eastwood, W.O.I F.F.; 42
Eastwood, Lt. Herbert David;41
Eatwell, W.O.I H.A.; 7
Eden, Lt. Michael C.; 53
Edwards, Lt. Donald Kenneth; 29
Edwards, Captain Edward James; 25
Egan, Captain Bernard Mary; 10
Elliott, Captain James Roland; 49
Ellis, Lt. Frederick William; 49
Ellis, W.O.II J.; 53
Erskine, Lt. James S.; 30
Evans, Lt. Kenneth Charles; 53
Evans, Lt. Philip Brandon; 29
Ewens, Captain Alfred Francis; 64

Farrands, Lt. Noel Frank; 47
Falck, Lt. Rudolph J.; 4
Faulkner-Brown, Captain Harry ; 53
Feltham, Lieutenant Robert Harold
    Bruce; 9
Fielding, W.O.II L.S.; 31
Fitch, Lt.-Col. John A.C.; 13
Fitzgerald, Lt. George Henry; 25
Flavell, 2Lt. James Sydney
    Channel; 10
Fleet, George; 24
Flockhart, Captain A.S.; 60
Fogarty, Lt. Christopher Winthrop; 44
Foot, Captain Reginald Sydney; 29
Forman, Major Michael Bertram; 37
Forshall, Captain Peter Hyde; 24
Foulkes, Lt. Ralph Colwyn; 40
Frank Captain Anthony Mutrie; 11

Fraser Lt. William A.; 13
Frazer, Major Simon Macleod; 61
Frost Lt-Col. John Dulton; 10

Galbraith, Lt. Doug; 40
Gardiner, Lieutenant Joseph; 8
Garnett, W.O.II A.; 47
Gatland, W.O.II G.; 24
Gavin, W.O.II P.E.; 60
Gay, W.O.I R.D. Gillespie; 17
Gell, Captain William Vincent
    Aloysius; 55
George, Captain Stephen; 52
Gex, Major G.F. de; 44
Gibbs, Captain Frederick Michael; 17
Gibbs, W.O.II W.; 55
Glick, Lieutenant B.J.; 9
Gilchrist, Major David Alexander; 25
Gillespie, Lt. S.; 13
Gilman, Captain E.I.; 50
Glassborow, Lt. Geoffrey William; 28
Godfrey, Lt. Arthur R.; 27
Godfrey, W.O.II Douglas Aubrey; 29
Golden, Captain Lewis Lawrence; 56
Glover, Lt. Joseph Winston; 21
Glover, Lt. Robert G.; 49
Goodman, W.O.II W.A.; 46
Gordon, Major Ronald Rodger; 59
Gough, Major Charles Frederick
    Howard `Freddie'; 39
Gourlay, Captain George Cleland; 38
Gow, Captain Roderick G.A.; 51
Graham-Jones, Captain John; 31
Grainger, W.O.II R.E.; 22
Gray, Captain William Buchanan; 4
Grayburn, Lt. John H.; 11
Green, Lt. Alan Thomas; 34
Green, Captain Michael Douglas; 52
Greenhalgh, Lt. Frederick Henry; 8
Gregg, Lt. Robert A.; 44, 57
Grice, Lt. John Derek; 55
Grieve, Captain Charles Gordon; 2
Griffin, Captain Peter; 6
Griffiths, Captain Tudor Morgan; 47
Griffiths, Sergeant W.; 19
Grimshaw, W.O.II Frederick A.; 33
Grose, Lt. William Albert P.; 25
Groves, Captain Philip Nigel; 7
Grubb, Captain Michael Wathing; 40
Guthrie, Lt. David Robert; 40
Guyon, Lieutenant George Edmund; 8
Hacart, Lt. Yves; 17

King, W.O.II A.J.; 9
King Captain Sir Frank Douglas; 24
Kipping, Lt. Albert E.; 38

Ladds, Lt. Frederick W.; 39
Lamb, W.O. I W.M. C.; 35
Lamond, Lt. William James
  Melville; 36
Lane, Major Thomas Benjamin; 28
Langford, Captain John Adair; 51
Lasenby, Lieutenant James Joseph; 8
Lashmore, W.O. II A.B.; 21
Lathbury, Brigadier Sir Gerald
  William; 6
Lawson, W.O.II David; 47
Lawson, Captain John; 60
Lea, Lt-Col. Sir George Harris; 23
Lee, Captain John Henry Dixon; 45
Leitch, Lt. Carmel S.; 46
Levien, Lt. Robert Hugh; 11
Lewis, Lt. John Thomas; 48
Lewis, Major Richard Peter Cecil; 15
Lickerish, Lt. Alexander A.; 39
Lindsay, Captain David; 47
Lindley, Major Francis William; 21
Linton, Major James Edward Fryer;46
Lipmann-Kessel, Captain Alexander
  William; 59
Livesey, Captain Trevor John; 53
Livingstone, Captain James
  Stewart; 38
Locke, Lt. Frederick John de
  Riveille; 16
Lockett, Lt. B.S.; 48
Loder-Symonds, Lieutenant-Colonel
  Robert Guy; 43
Lockyer, Captain Leslie Arthur
  George; 26
Logan, Captain James Watt; 10, 62
Longden, Lt. David Gordon; 27
Longland, Major Cedric James; 59
Lonsdale, Major Richard Thomas
  Henry; 23
Lord, W.O.I J.C.; 13
Lott W.O.II G.H.; 22
Louis, Captain Percy; 60

MacDonnell, Lt. Charles James; 28
MacDonald, Lt. George Smith; 37
MacDonald, Lt. John James M.; 29
Mackay, Captain Eric MacLachlan; 53
MacKenzie, Lt. Alexander; 35

Mackenzie, Lieutenant-Colonel Charles
  Baillie; 2
MacKenzie, Lt. P.B.; 22
Mackey, Lt. P.W.A.; 22
Madden, Major David John; 2
Maguire, Major Hugh Pownall; 2
Mallet, Captain William John; 51
Manley, Captain Bernard Vincent; 42
Manning, Lt. Geoffrey; 64
Mansfield, Captain Peter Geoffrey
  Alan; 8
Marquand, Captain Wilfred
  James; 6, 57
Marriott, W.O.II E.S.J.; 53
Marshall, 2/Lt. George Christopher; 43,
  57
Marshall, Lt. John Wilson; 40
Marrable, Lt-Col. Arthur Trevor; 61
Martin, W.O.II E.G.B.; 8
Martin, Captain Victor David
  Randall; 44, 63
Mason, Lt. Peter Brown; 38
Matthews, Lt. Harold Theodore
  Bernhardt; 16
Mawson, Captain Stuart Radcliffe; 23,
  62
McBishop, 2/Lt. H.I.; 24
McCardie, Lt-Col. William Derek
  Hessing; 27
McCartney, Lt. John Stewart
  Granville; 32
McCombe, Captain D.W.; 2
McCooke, Captain John Brewster; 28
McCormie, Captain J.J.; 53
McCourt, Captain James Frederik; 37
McDermont Lt. A.J.; 11
McFadden, Lieutenant John T.; 9
McFarlane, Lt. P.; 48
McGladdery, W.O.II A.B.; 33
McGowan, Captain Daniel; 58
McInnes, Lt. W.; 49
McKenna, Lt. James L.; 24
McKinnon, W.O.II N.; 18
McLean Captain Donald W.; 10
McLaren, Lt. Robert L.; 49
McLeod, Captain N.; 48
McMillen, Captain Christopher John
  S.; 51
McNabb, Lt. Trevor V.R.; 39
McNaught, Lt. Eustace Arthur; 48
Meadows, W.O.II G.C.; 39
Meads, W.O.II Dennis; 11

Meikle, Lt. Ian O.; 45
Meish, Lt. J.L.; 51
Menzies, Captain Alistair Charles
　　Vass; 17
Miller, Captain Cecil Ralph; 6
Miller, Major Joseph Esmond; 3, 58
Miller, Captain Thomas Visger; 50
Milo, Major Peter Middleton; 25
Mobbs, Lt-Col. Gerald Hubrey; 3, 42
Monsell Lt. John Humphrey Arnold; 11
Montgomery, Captain H.; 19
Montgomery, Major T.E.; 33
Moore, Lt. Francis Pepys Durie; 47
Morgan, W.O.II Leskie; 26
Morgan, W.O.II T.E.V.; 46
Morris, W.O.II D.; 24
Morrisey, Major Dennis Richard
　　Lawrence; 31
Morrison, Captain James Gilbert; 35
Morley, Lt. Wilfred David `Wilf'
　　Clarence; 4
Mortlock, Captain Douglas Gerald; 6
Morton Captain Richard Elwin; 12
Moy-Thomas, Captain Edward A.; 26
Munford, Major Dennis Stewart; 47
Murray, Lt. Alexander D.M.; 37
Murray, Major Douglas Campbell; 52
Myers, Lt-Col. Edmund Charles Wolf
　　`Eddie'; 52

Naylor, Captain John Denis; 55
Neill, Major William; 34
Newport, Lt. Edward Selwyn; 32
Newton-Dunn, Major Owen Frank; 2
Nicholson, W.O.II J.R.; 8
Noble, Lt. Jeffrey Fraser; 18
Norman-Walker, Major Arthur
　　Fairfax; 45
Norwood, Lt. Carlisle; 29
Novel, Lt. C.B.; 60

O'Callaghan, Captain E.C.; 54
O'Grady, Captain Arthur Edgar; 50
Olliff, Lt. Donald Edwin; 60
Osbourne, Lt. G.; 55
O'Sullivan, Captain John Charles; 9
Oxley, W.O. II L.E.; 9

Page, Major Michael; 17
Panter, Captain Stanley Charles; 11
Palmer, Lt. Cyril; 49
Park, Captain John R.C.R.; 40

Parker, Lt. D.; 27
Pascal, Lt. Alan F.; 40
Paull, Lt George Arthur; 49
Payton-Reid, Lt.-Col. Robert; 35
Pearson, Lt. Herbert E.; 39
Pearson, Lt. Roderick Percy; 44
Pelissier, Lt. Charles Marius; 36
Peele, Lt. Richard de Courcy; 25
Percival, Captain Arthur; 7, 62
Perkins, Major Aeneas John
　　Martin; 53
Perrin-Brown, Major Christopher; 9
Perse , Captain Peter John; 25
Philip, Major John Etherington; 30
Philips, Capt. Edward Leigh;
Platt, Captain Horace A.; 39
Polley, Lt. David Arthur; 56
Poole, Captain Harry; 39
Pope, W.O.I Albert; 31
Potesta, W.O.I W.; 56
Pott, Major Robert Laslett John; 19
Powell, Major Geoffrey Stewart; 19
Preston, Herbert OBE; 3
Proctor, Lt. John Richard; 22
Pruden, W.O.II E.E.; 59
Pryce, Lt. John Ivor; 14

Queripel, Captain Lionel E.; 22

Radcliff, Lt. Herbert C.N.; 21
Randall, Lt. Derrick Henry; 43, 63
Read, Sergeant E.; 18
Redman, Captain Theodore Francis;60
Reed, Sgt. A.E.; 45
Reed, W.O.I Matty; 64
Reese, Captain Robert Miles
　　Anthony; 32
Reynolds, Lt. Jack; 28
Riches, W.O.II A.F.; 24
Richey, Captain James Alexander
　　Dodwell; 9
Ridler, Captain D.H.; 59
Rigby-Jones, Major Guy; 61
Ritson, Major Ernest V.; 17
Roberts, Lt. Harry R.; 64
Robertson-Durham, Lt. Alexander
　　Weir; 36
Roberts, Lt. Alan Douglas; 34
Roberts Lieutenant Andrew; 6
Roberts, Captain Graham Chatfield; 2
Robertson, Lt. Richard A.; 53
Robson, Lt. Peter Thorp; 56

Robson, Captain Donald Hotham; 26
Robinson, Captain Sir Wilfred Henry
    Frederick; 15
Robinson, W.O.II William; 29
Roderick, Lt. H.C.J.; 20
Roebuck, Lt. Ernest; 30
Rogers, Captain Terence P.W.; 19
Rogerson, Lt. James F.; 24
Rose. Captain T.; 44
Rowell, Captain John J.; 31
Royall, Lt. Anthony Robert; 33
Russell, Lt. David Edward Charles; 12
Russell, Lt. John Alexander; 12
Rutherford, Captain John; 13, 62
Ryall, Lt. Geoffrey; 48

Sackville, Lord Buckhurst, Lt. W.H.; 16
Sankey, Lt. Crofton Edmund Peter; 52
Saunders, Lt. Peter; 22
Schwartz, Lt. Ralph Harding; 27
Scott, Captain George Barton
    Douglas; 61
Scott, W.O.II William W.; 11
Scott-Malden, Captain Charles Peter; 2
Scrivenr, Lt. Edmund Filford; 33
Seeckts, W.O.II J.; 13
Seccombe Captain Ernest Walter; 13
Sharp,Lt. Roland; 29
Sharlpes, Lt. Arthur D.L.; 36
Shaw, Lt. Edward Ernest; 48
Sheriff, Major Charles Gordon; 38
Siely,W.O.I J.; 44
Siggins, Lt. Donald Cecil Clifford; 44
Silverster, Captain Vernon John Ballis;
    17
Simpson, Lt. Denis Jackson; 53
Simmons, Captain Clifford Alan; 61
Simonds, Major John Mallor; 27
Skilton, Lt. Douglas Henry; 31
Skinner, Lt. William Henderson; 54
Slater, W.O.I D.; 27
Smith, Captain Dennis Dale; 21
Smith, Captain James Gordon
    Anstruther; 53
Smith Major Peter; 60
Smith, Captain John Raymond; 56
Smith, W.O.II S.; 25
Smith, Lt. Thomas Joseph Arthur; 4
Smyth, Lt-Col. Kennth B.I.; 20
Spivey, Captain Robert Edward; 41
Speller, Lt. Cecil Edmund Kirby; 41
Speke, 2/Lt. Wilfred H.; 25

Squire, W.O.II R.; 21
Staddon, Lt. Roy Glinn; 54
Stanford Lt. Colin Macdonald; 12
Stainford, Lt. Peter; 63
Stayton, W.O.II L.J.; 36
Steel, Lt. James; 54
Steer, Captain George William; 36
Strang, Lt. James H.; 37
Stephenson, Lt-Col. Thomas Godfrey
    Vaughan; 56
Stevens, Captain Raymond H.; 50
Stevenson, Lt. John; 40
Steward, W.O.II J.; 41
Stewart, Major Richard Henry; 32
Stott, Lt. William Patrick; 33
Storrs, Lt. David Valentine; 52
St. John Packe, Lt-Col. Michael; 55
Strachan, W.O.I G.A.; 10
Stark, Major Ronald Leslie; 9
Stringer, W.O.II George Henry; 34
Stroud, W.O.II E.D.; 19
Suter, Lt. Douglas John; 17
Sutton, Lieutenant William John
    Fisher; 8
Swanston, W.O.II J.; 38
Swinscow, Captain Thomas Douglas
    Victor; 39, 63
Sykes, W.O.II W.S.; 19

Tannenbaum, Lt. A.L.; 10
Tasker, W.O.II D.R.; 12
Tate, Major Francis R.; 10
Tate, Lt. Joseph; 32
Tatham-Warter Major Allison Digby;
    11
Taylor, Captain Basil Anthony
    Bethune; 46
Taylor, Captain Derek John; 16
Taylor, Lt. Hugh Gilson; 16
Taylor, Lt. James William; 29, 38
Taylor, Captain John Cuthill; 61
Taylor, Captain Percy Albert; 46
Taylor, Captain Willie Andrew; 6
Temple, Captain Reginald Robert; 16
Thessiger, Captain Roderic Miles
    Doughty; 14
Thomas, Lt. Anthony R.; 26
Thomas, Lt. Norman Leslie B.; 54
Thomas, Lt. Reginald L.; 24
Thompson, Lt-Col. William Francis
    Kynaston `Sheriff`; 44
Thorne, Captain Selwyn; 44

Thyer, W.O.II Herbert; 34

Tiernan, Lt. John; 61

Timmins, Lt. Roy E.J.W.; 54

Timothy, Major John; 8

Tobin, Captain John James Walton; 59

Tower, Major Philip Thomas; 43

Townsend, Lt-Col. Eric; 59

Trehearn, Lt. Leslie Edward Sidney; 21

Trotman, Captain A.; 44

Turner, W.O.II Ronald A.; 64

Turrell, Lieutenant Albert Thomas; 7

Turner, Lt. Philip Hart; 29

Twidle,Lt. Victor Ray; 17

Twist, W.O.II V.J.; 19

Urquhart, Major General Robert Elliot
    `Roy'; 2

Ursell, W.O.II N.; 32

Vedeniapine, Lt. Alexis Peter; 13

Voeux, Lt.-Col.– Sir William Richard
    de Bacquencourtdes; 17

Viasto, Lt. Robert Alexander; 11

Vickers, Lt. Arthur Andrew; 25

Waddy, Major Alexander Peter H.; 14

Waddy, Major John Liewellyn; 19

Wadsworth, Lt. John Graham Hilton;
    39

Wainwright, Captain Thomas James;
    18

Wallis, Major David W.; 10

Walpole, Lt. Robert Holland; 53

Walters, Lt. Ernest Frederick; 27

Walker, John Waine; 45

Warrack, Col. Graeme Matthaw; 3, 58

Warr, Major Peter Esmond; 22

Watling, Lt. Stanley E.; 22

Watson, W.O.II A.; 14

Watson, Sgt. Thomas; 33

Wayte, Lt. Albert E.F.; 38

Webber, Major Daniel Robert
    Wyndham; 24

Welch, Captain W. Gordon; 34

Wetherill, Captain Peter Hindley; 54

Welbelove, Lt. John Arthur; 33

Wells, Captain Charles Edward C.; 59

White, W.O.I G.; 20

Whitley, W.O.II J.; 8

Whimister, Captain William Swanson;
    50

White, Lt. Kenneth Grayston; 46

Whittaker, Lt. Harry; 48

Willock, Lt. N.R.; 19

Widdicombe, Lt. John Wicks; 47

Widdowson, Major George G.; 20

Wight-Boycott, Major R.D.; 51

Wilkinson, Lt. Peter William; 47

Willcocks, Captain Arthur Hambly; 28

Williams, Lieutenant John Liewellyn;
    7

Williams, W.O.II V.; 28

Wilson, Captain Baldwin; 33

Wilson, Major Bernard Alexander
    `Boy'; 41

Wilson, Lt. Robert Finlay; 35

Winchester, Major John Chisholm; 54

Winter-Goodman, Captain; 55

Wise, Lt. Edgar Gerald; 54

Withecombe, Lt. Eric; 49

Withers, Lt. Leonard; 28

Withnall, Lt. William Charles; 28

Wood, Lt. R.; 25

Wood, Lt. Ronald W.; 19

Woods, Lt. James H.; 46

Woods, Lt. R.B.; 11

Woodward, Captain Geoffrey Calvin;
    28

Wright, Captain David; 62

Wright, Lt. Leonard William; 25

Wright, Major Philip Richard Thomas;
    29

Wyss, Captain Ernest Mariel; 30

Related Books by Travelogue 219:

www.tl219.com

Angel of Arnhem: Casualties of the 1st Airborne Division buried in the back garden of Jan and Kate ter Horst, the old Rectory, Benedorpsweg, Oosterbeek 18-26 September 1944 by Philip Reinders
ISBN: 978-1-927679-16-6

Market Garden Engineer Series by John Sliz: (www.stormboatkings.ca)

The Wrong Side of the River:
The Polish Engineer Company at Arnhem
ISBN: 978-09783838-0-0

Basic Function:
The 4th Parachute Squadron, Royal Engineers at Arnhem
ISBN: 978-0-9783838-1-7

Engineers at the Bridge:
The 1st Parachute Squadron Royal Engineers at Arnhem
ISBN: 978-0-9783838-4-8

Assault Boats On The Waal:
The 307th Engineer Battalion During Operation Market Garden
ISBN: 978-0-9877404-5-8

Bridging Hell's Highway:
The 326th Engineer Battalion During Operation Market Garden
ISBN: 978-0-9783838-6-2

A Long Tradition:
The 9th (Airborne) Field Company Royal Engineers at Arnhem
ISBN: 978-09877404-4-1

A Token Force:
The 261st Field Park Company Royal Engineers (Airborne) at Arnhem
ISBN: 978-0-9877404-6-5

Commander Royal Engineers:
The Headquarters of the Royal Engineers at Arnhem
ISBN: 978-1-92679-04-3

Bridging the Club Route:
Guards Armoured Division's Engineers During Operation Market Garden
ISBN: 978-1-927679-14-2

22540246R00047

Printed in Great Britain
by Amazon